ULTIMATE
COVER
LETTERS

1 2

ULTIMATE
COVER
LETTERS

FOURTH EDITION

A guide to job search letters, online
applications and follow-up strategies

MARTIN JOHN YATE

LONDON PHILADELPHIA NEW DELHI

First published in the United States in 1992 as *Cover Letters that Knock 'em Dead* by Adams Media Corporation

First published in Great Britain in 2003 as *The Ultimate Job Search Letters Book* by Kogan Page Limited
Reprinted in 2007
Second edition published in 2008 as *Ultimate Cover Letters*
Third edition 2012
Fourth edition 2015
Reprinted 2015 (twice)

Published by arrangement with Adams Media Corporation, 57 Littlefield Street, Avon, MA 02322, USA

2nd Floor, 45 Gee Street
London EC1V 3RS
United Kingdom
www.koganpage.com

1518 Walnut Street, Suite 1100
Philadelphia PA 19102
USA

4737/23 Ansari Road
Daryaganj
New Delhi 110002
India

© Martin John Yate, 1992, 1995, 1998, 2001, 2002, 2003, 2008, 2012, 2015

ISBN   978 0 7494 7453 9

British Library Cataloguing-in-Publication Data

A CIP record for this book is available from the British Library.

Typeset by Graphicraft Limited, Hong Kong
Print production managed by Jellyfish
Printed and bound by CPI Group (UK) Ltd, Croydon CR0 4YY

CONTENTS

READ THIS FIRST

At every stage of your job search, letters can help you make important points that can be difficult to express verbally. Use the strategies and tactics I'll show you in this book to position yourself as someone worth taking seriously.

Selling yourself with the written word is always a challenge. And with everything you have to stay on top of in your professional life, packaging yourself in job search letters is probably one thing you haven't made a priority.

But the writing skills displayed in your letters and CVs can have a *major* impact on your job search. Ignore developing these critical skills and you can stay longer in that going-nowhere job, or be longer unemployed.

This book has helped millions of people around the world craft hard-hitting letters that helped them win interviews and job offers. It can do the same for you.

You'll find job search letters of every conceivable type here: from cover letters to follow-up after telephone and face-to-face meetings, networking, resurrection, acceptance, rejection, and those oh-so-happy letters of resignation.

These letters work, giving you an edge in a highly competitive job market. They are *real* letters that have already worked in someone's job search. Some of these letters I've helped people write, others have been sent to me by career coaches, professional CV writers, headhunters, HR managers and grateful readers. They will work for you too when you customize them to your own unique circumstances and your voice. What do I mean by 'your voice'? I mean that as you learn to customize and create your own letters, they will work best when the tone of the letter sounds natural, and that means staying away from words you wouldn't normally use in a professional context.

Throughout this book the words 'mail', 'letter', and 'e-mail' are intended to be interchangeable, unless otherwise noted. Written communications can be delivered by either e-mail or traditional mail, with the majority now going by e-mail. However, I don't want you to ignore traditional mail, because when you do something other job hunters aren't doing, you stand out.

How recruitment works

A good cover letter and subsequent follow-up letters can speed your application through the four stages all employers go through in the recruitment screening and selection cycle. They won't win you the job in and of themselves but they can make a big difference to the way you are perceived as a professional and as a person, thus differentiating you from the competition.

The four stages are:

1 *Long-list development.* The first stage of most recruitment strategies is to develop a 'long list' of 10–12 potential candidates.

2 *Short-list development.* The long list of candidates is screened for best-fit-to-the-job, reducing the long list to four or six candidates. Those who make the cut become the 'short list' and are invited in for an interview, after first passing the additional screening of a telephone interview. A folder is created for each candidate, including both print and electronic documents.

3 *Short-list prioritization.* Through a series of interviews, usually one, two, or three, the short-list candidates are ranked for ability and fit.

4 *Short-list review and decision.* Each candidate's folder is reviewed for one last time before the final decision. The folder will include your CV, the employer's notes, and any cover and follow-up letters you have been smart enough to send during the interview process. These letters make additional points, clear up mistakes and omissions, and brand you as a competent professional and real human being who would be a pleasure to work with.

In each of the recruitment and selection steps you will pass through in pursuit of your next step up the professional ladder, letters have a role to play in separating you from other candidates (part of a process called professional branding) and easing your passage through each step of the selection cycle. Letters support your application and remind employers of your relevant skills, professionalism, continued existence, and interest and suitability for the job, all the way through to the offer.

Any experienced headhunter will tell you that when there are no major differences between two top candidates, the offer will always go to the most intelligently enthusiastic; your letters can help make that intelligent enthusiasm clear to your prospective employer.

Each step of the interview cycle presents you with significant opportunities to advance your application. You can add additional information after a meeting, clear up a misunderstanding or a poor answer ('I'm good at my job, but not so good at

interviews, just haven't had that many. When we were talking about _____
perhaps I didn't make it clear that …').

By reading this book and then mining the sample letters provided, you can take a phrase from this letter and a few words from another to create unique letters that reflect the real you.

Because your comments are in a letter, it speaks for you when you aren't there to speak for yourself; a strong written dimension to your job search can double your effectiveness. The different types of letters you create during the interview cycle demonstrate your writing skills, attention to detail, professionalism, and that all-important enthusiasm. Each letter adds another meaningful plus to your application.

With this book on your desk, you won't waste time creating letters from scratch, and once settled in a new position, you can apply these same strategies and tactics to the written communications that are an integral part of every successful career.

1

Cover letters: the secret weapon in your job search

A recent survey of 1,000 executives revealed that 91 per cent found cover letters to be valuable in their evaluation of candidates. Your letter can add information that isn't in your CV and help to establish a communication channel between two professionals with a common interest.

You can write the greatest cover letter in the world but if you don't learn how to use it properly, your job search will take longer and the job you get may not be the best you deserve. Cover letters are most effective when you develop a plan of attack that includes reaching out directly to employers. Whenever someone in a position to hire you reads your CV and cover letter, the odds of getting that interview increase dramatically, because you have skipped right over the initial hurdle – getting pulled from the CV database – and you are speaking directly to the hiring authority.

The primary goal of every job search is to get into conversations, as quickly and frequently as possible, with people in a position to hire you; without conversations, job offers can't be made. Difficulty reaching employers with your message is one of the major reasons why many job searches stall. This happens when job searchers involve themselves, almost exclusively, with posting CVs to CV banks and responding to job postings by uploading CVs into other CV databases.

However, when you can get your CV, personalized with a cover letter, in front of employers, you differentiate yourself and substantially increase your chances of landing an interview.

Employers overwhelmingly appreciate cover and follow-up letters. If all you are planning to do is load your CV into CV databases, a cover letter can still help. Its main strength is in personalizing your message to a specific company and ideally a specific person. When you develop a plan of attack for your job search that includes reaching out directly to decision makers, the personalizing touch of a letter really increases your impact.

The job titles to target during your job search are:

- Those job titles most likely to be in a position to hire you. Usually this will be managers one to three levels above your target job.

- Those job titles most likely to be involved in the selection process. Usually this will be managers working in related departments, recruitment and HR. Whenever you have a name in one of these disciplines, use a letter to stand out.

Your ideal target for direct communication is always someone who can hire you, although any management title offers opportunity for referral. Even Human Resources contacts are valuable. They can't make the hiring decision, but the pivotal nature of HR jobs means the professionals in this area are aware of all areas within a company that could use your skills.

Any name and title you capture in a job search is valuable. With the internet at your fingertips there are countless ways to identify the names of people who hold the titles you need to reach, and if a name and title is of no use to you, it might be just the contact another job hunter needs, so it can be a valuable commodity to develop in your networking activities.

When an e-mail or envelope is opened, your cover letter will be the first thing looked at. It personalizes your application for a specific job in ways that are impossible for your CV to do, given its impersonal structure. The cover letter sets the stage for the reader to accept your CV, and therefore you, as something and someone special. It can create common ground between you and the reader and demonstrate that you are well qualified and suitable for *this* job and *this* company.

Six tactics that help your cover letter work

Address your target by name

Your first step is to grab the reader's attention and arouse interest, so whenever possible address the letter to someone by name.

Approaching employers directly is one of the very best tactics for getting job offers. Whenever you can find the names of any one of the titles involved in the recruitment and selection cycle, approach them directly and address them by name.

Make your letter readable

Your customer, the reader, is always going to be distracted, so your letters need to be easily readable, focused, clear and brief. Your letters should be succinct as well as both friendly and respectful; they should never be unfocused, pompous or sound like you swallowed a dictionary. You can also grab the reader's attention with the appearance of your letter, which should mirror the fonts and font sizes of your CV, giving you a co-ordinated and professional look.

Hardly anyone in a position to hire you is still young enough to read 10-point fonts comfortably. Anyone who has been staring at computer screens for 10 or more years and has 10 other priorities pressing for attention is likely to have problems with tiny font sizes and elaborate but unreadable fonts. I recommend a minimum of 11- or 12-point font size (more on this later).

Applying these rules of matching font and font size to *e-mail and print* letters is easy to do and yet easily overlooked; but paying attention to the details pays dividends in any job search.

Emphasize your personal brand

Branding is the process by which you consistently draw attention to the bundle of skills and behaviours that make you a little different. All the job search letters you send – and yes, that includes every e-mail – are part of the packaging that captures you. If your written words look good, carry a succinct, relevant, readily accessible message, and show you to be a professional with a clear sense of self, you're well on the road to establishing a viable professional brand. When your actions differentiate you from others, your standing as a candidate is improved.

What makes you special?

- Being smart enough to get your CV directly under the nose of a manager, who just wants to make a good decision and get back to work, makes you special.

- Getting your CV to the manager in a creative way and showing that you know what you are doing makes you special. Your letter might say in part, 'I sent my CV by e-mail but thought you might appreciate a screen break, so you'll find it attached to this letter...'. In that case, your e-mail should say, 'As well as attaching my CV to this e-mail, in case you need a screen break I've also sent it by traditional mail.'

- Writing a strong cover letter that presents your CV and establishes connectivity between you and the manager makes you special.

- Keeping your message clear and succinct makes you special.

- Following up your meetings with thoughtful letters that continue the messaging of a consummate professional makes you special and confirms your professional status.

- Making sure in all your e-mails and printed letters that the fonts are legible and coordinated with your CV makes you special.

Continuity in written communication

To ensure continuity in all your written communications:

1 Make the font you employ for contact information and headlines in both your CV and your cover letter the same.

2 Use the same font you choose for your CV's body copy for the message in your letter.

3 Use the same font choices for all your e-mail communications. Smart idea: set the chosen font as your default e-mail font.

4 Make the font you use in your written communications consistent with the font you use in your e-mail and other online communications.

5 Get matching paper for CV, cover letters and envelopes. Every office superstore has them. Sending your cover letter and CV by traditional mail when the opportunity arises is a way to get your CV read because most job hunters don't think to do this. Today, managers get far fewer CVs by mail, but busy managers still like a break from the computer screen so more time is spent on your CV.

Be succinct and on-message

A good cover letter gets your CV read with serious concentration. Time is precious. Recruiters and managers won't waste it on a letter that rambles. Your letter should always reflect a professional whose CV has something to say.

When you can, make a specific reference to a job's key requirements. You want the reader to move from your letter to the CV already thinking that here's a candidate who can do this job. You can do this in either of two ways:

- referring to a job's most important requirements;

- referring to the issues behind the job's most important requirements.

If an advertisement, a job posting or a telephone conversation with a potential employer reveals an aspect of a particular job opening that is not addressed in your CV (and for some reason you haven't had time to update it), use a cover letter to fill in the gaps. The Executive Briefing (you'll see a sample shortly) is an especially useful tool for this job.

Brevity is important. The letter doesn't sell everything about you – that's the CV's job. Rather, the letter positions you for serious conversation, with luck demonstrating that you grasp what's at the heart of the job, leaving your reader wanting more.

End with a call to action

Just as you worked to create a strong opening, make sure your closing carries the same conviction. It is the reader's last personal impression of you, so make it strong, make it tight, and make it obvious that you are serious about entering into meaningful conversation. Your letters should always include a call to action. Explain when, where and how you can be contacted. You can also be proactive, telling the reader that you intend to follow up a certain point in time if they have not contacted you.

Every step of the job search and selection cycle offers opportunities to use letters to promote your application. A good, strong letter will get your foot in the door, differentiate you from other contenders, and ultimately help you define a distinctive professional brand. Although the majority of your communications will be e-mails, stand out by sending really important information in both e-mails and traditional letters. If nothing more, your important communication gets read twice which increases the odds of you being noticed.

The six types of
job search letters

Wholesale adoption of the internet as the primary recruitment vehicle has completely changed the way you need to approach the job search.

Every year the number of CVs loaded into commercial CV databases grows exponentially. Currently the larger databases each house more than 36 million CVs. Many individual CV banks have over 1 million CVs stored, and social networking sites like LinkedIn have over 70 million CVs and professional profiles registered. This has made life easier for recruiters, since they can usually find enough qualified candidates in the top 20 CVs from any database, and given the large number of potential candidates, they rarely dig deeper.

In the CV databases that allow attachments to your CV, a cover letter helps you stand out by making additional and supportive comments about your capabilities. When you send your CV directly to a potential employer by using their name and title, your CV and cover letter have even greater impact because you can differentiate yourself by addressing the manager or recruiter by name and by customizing your message and most importantly, you sidestep the CV database entirely.

Here are six types of cover letters that will help your job search. Each is a composite letter I built from scouring the examples that appear later in the book, taking a word from one example and a phrase from another. In each example, I have underlined the borrowed phrases to give you an idea of how easy it is to create your own original documents with a little cutting and pasting. The six letters are:

1 The cover letter for when you do not know of a specific job but have the name of someone to send the letter to or are uploading to a CV bank where you can attach it to your CV.

2 The executive briefing. A very effective cover letter for when you have knowledge of the job's requirements, especially when you can address it to someone by name.

3 A cover letter in response to an online job posting.

4 A cover letter aimed at headhunters.

5 A networking letter for getting the word out to the professional community about your search.

6 A broadcast letter if your CV doesn't quite fit the job.

A cover letter when you do not know of a specific job opening

This letter is designed to be uploaded to a database as an attachment or sent to a potential employer whose name you've garnered from your research. Of course, if you are sending this to an individual it should be personalized with a salutation and include references to the company, some detail of the job, or the establishment of some common ground between you and the recipient.

When you do not know of a specific job opening

James Sharpe
1 Any Street • Anytown, AA1 1AA
12345 678901

2 October 20–

Jackson Bethell, Director of Operations
DataLink Products
111 Any Avenue
Anytown, AA1 1AA

Dear Jackson Bethell,

Recently I have been researching the leading local companies in data communications. My search has been for companies that are respected in the field and that provide ongoing training programmes. The name of DataLink Products keeps coming up as a top company.

I am an experienced voice and data communications specialist with a substantial background in IBM environments. If you have an opening for someone in this area, you will see that my CV demonstrates a person of unusual dedication, efficiency and drive. My experience and achievements include:

- the complete redesign of a data communications network, projected to increase efficiency company-wide by 12 per cent;

- the installation and troubleshooting of a Defender IV call-back security system for a dial-up network.

I enclose a copy of my CV, and look forward to exploring any of the ways you feel my background and skills would benefit DataLink Products. While I prefer not to use my employer's time taking personal calls at work, with discretion I can be reached at 10987 654321 to initiate contact. However, I would rather you call me at _____ in the evening. Let's talk!

Yours sincerely,

James Sharpe

James Sharpe

When you do not know of a specific job opening

JANE SWIFT
1 Any Street, Anytown, AA1 1AA
12345 678901

David Doors, Director of Marketing   14 January 20–
Martin Financial Group
111 Any Avenue
Anytown, AA1 1AA

Dear David Doors,

I have always followed the performance of your company in *Mutual Funds Newsletter.*

Recently your notice regarding a Market Analyst in *Investor's Business Daily* caught my eye – and your company name caught my attention. Your record over the last three years shows exceptional portfolio management. Because of my experience with one of your competitors, I know I could make significant contributions.

I would like to talk to you about your personnel needs and how I am able to contribute to your department's goals.

An experienced market analyst, I have an economics background (MA London) and a strong quantitative analysis approach to market fluctuations. This combination has enabled me to consistently pick the new technology flotations that are the backbone of the growth-orientated mutual fund. For example:

I first recommended XYZ Fund six years ago. More recently my clients have been strongly invested in ABC Growth (in the high-risk category), and DEF Growth and Income (for the cautious investor). Those following my advice over the last six years have consistently outperformed the market.

I know that CVs help you sort out the probables from the possibles, but they are no way to judge the personal calibre of an individual. I would like to meet you and demonstrate that along with the credentials, I have the professional commitment that makes for a successful team player.

Yours sincerely,

Jane Swift

Jane Swift

The executive briefing

The executive briefing is a different and effective form of cover letter to use *whenever you have information about a job opening* – perhaps from an online job posting, a lead, or a conversation with one of your network contacts – and there is a good skill match. The executive briefing gets right to the point and makes life easy for the reader. It introduces your CV, as well as customizing and supplementing it. Why is an executive briefing so effective?

1 It quickly matches job requirements against the skills you bring to the table, making analysis much easier for the reader and a successful outcome more likely for you.

2 While an initial screener (someone who quickly sorts through cover letters and CVs to separate the wheat from the chaff) may not have an in-depth understanding of the job's requirements, the executive briefing simplifies things by matching the job's requirements point-by-point to your abilities.

3 The executive briefing allows you to emphasize your skills in a particular area or fill any gaps in your CV with job-specific information.

4 If an opportunity comes along that is right for you but your CV isn't up to date or doesn't have the right focus, the executive briefing allows you to update your work history. This very professional quick fix is a godsend when someone asks to see your CV but it isn't up to date.

The executive briefing ensures that each CV you send out addresses the job's specific needs. It provides a comprehensive picture of a thorough professional, plus a personalized, fast, and easy-to-read synopsis that details exactly how your background matches the job description.

A cover letter in response to an online job posting

If you are writing as a result of an online job posting, you should mention both the website and any reference codes associated with the job:

'I read your job posting on your company's website on 5th January and felt I had to respond…'

'Your online job posting regarding a _____ on _____.com caught my eye, and your company name caught my attention.'

'This e-mail, and my attached CV, is in response to your job posting on _____.'

An executive briefing e-mail

From:	top10acct@anyserver.co.uk
To:	Recipient's e-mail address
Cc:	
Subject:	**Re: Accounting Manager**

Dear Recipient's Name,

I have nine years' accounting experience and am responding to your recent posting for an Accounting Manager on Careerbuilder. Please allow me to highlight my skills as they relate to your stated requirements.

Your Requirements	**My Experience**
Accounting degree, four years' experience	Obtained a degree in 2000 and have over four years' experience as an Accounting Manager
Excellent people skills and leadership	Effectively managed a staff of 24; ability to motivate staff, including supervisors
Strong administrative skills	Assisted in the development of a base reference skills-library with Microsoft Excel for 400 clients
Good communication skills	Trained new supervisors and staff via daily coaching sessions, communication meetings and technical skill sessions

My CV, pasted below and attached in MSWord, will flesh out my general background. I hope this executive briefing helps you use your time effectively today. I am ready to make a move. I hope we can talk soon.

Yours sincerely,

Joe Black

012345 67890
Attachment: CV

E-mail response to online job posting
(legal administrator)

From: Helen Darvik [darviklegalpro@earthlink.net]
To: Recipient's e-mail address
Cc:
Subject: Administrator/mgmnt/mktg/cmptr/acctg/planning/personnel

Dear Recipient's Name,

I am responding to your job posting on Hotjobs.com for a legal administrator of a law firm. I wrote to you on (date) about law administrator positions in the _____ area. I have attached another CV of my educational background and employment history. I am very interested in this position.

I have been a legal administrator for two law firms during the past six years. In addition, I have been a law firm consultant for over a year. Besides my law firm experience, I have been a medical administrator for over 10 years. I believe that all of this experience will enable me to manage the law firm for this position very successfully. I possess the management, marketing, computer, accounting/budgeting, financial planning, personnel, and people-orientated skills that will have a very positive impact on this law firm.

I will be in the _____ area later in the month, and hope we can meet at that time to discuss this position. I look forward to hearing from you, Ms _____, concerning this position. Thank you for your time and consideration.

Yours sincerely,

Helen Darvik
12345 678901
Attachment: CV

Recruitment agencies and executive recruiter

Headhunters deserve your respect. They are, after all, the most sophisticated salespeople in the world – they alone sell products that talk back! A headhunter will be only faintly amused by your exhortations 'to accept the challenge' or 'test your skills by finding me a job' in the brief moment before s/he throws your letter in the waste bin.

When approaching and working with headhunters – whether they are working for the local employment agency or a retained search firm – bear in mind these two rules and you won't go far wrong:

1 Tell the truth. Answer questions truthfully and you will likely receive help. Get caught in a lie and you will have established a career-long distrust with someone who probably possesses a very diverse and influential list of contacts.

2 Cut immediately to the chase in your letters and conversations. For example:

> *'I am forwarding my CV because I understand you specialize in representing employers in the _____ field.'*

> *'Please find the enclosed CV. As a specialist in the _____ field, I felt you might be interested in the skills of a _____.'*

> *'Among your many clients there may be one or two who are seeking an experienced professional for a position as a _____.'*

Remember that a cover letter sent to executive search firms and employment agencies, should mention your salary and, if appropriate, your geographic considerations.

An example of a cover letter you might send to a recruitment agency is on page 14.

Letter to a recruitment agency

James Sharpe
1 Any Street • Anytown, AA1 1AA
12345 678901

2 December 20–

Dear Mr O'Flynn,

I am forwarding my CV, as I understand that you specialize in the accounting profession. As you may be aware, the management structure at _____ will be reorganized in the near future. While I am enthusiastic about the future of the agency under its new leadership, I have elected to make this an opportunity for change and professional growth.

My many years of experience lend themselves to a finance management position in any medium-sized service firm, but I am open to other opportunities. Although I would prefer to remain in London, I would entertain other areas of the country, if the opportunity warrants it. I am currently earning £65,000 a year.

I have enclosed my CV for your review. Should you be conducting a search for someone with my background at the present time or in the near future, I would greatly appreciate your consideration. I would be happy to discuss my background more fully with you on the phone or at a personal interview.

Yours sincerely,

James Sharpe

James Sharpe

Enclosure: CV

Networking letters

Nothing works like a personal recommendation from a fellow professional. It is no accident that successful people in all fields know each other, or at least know *of* each other. You get the most out of networking by being connected to your profession and the professionals within it.

There are important considerations to bear in mind with networking letters:

1 Establish connectivity. Recall the last memorable contact you had with the person or mention someone that you have both spoken to recently. Use past employers, membership of professional associations, common interests or a topical event as a bridge builder.

If you are writing (and calling) as the result of a referral, say so and quote the person's name if appropriate:

> *'I am writing because our mutual colleague, John Stanovich, felt my skills and abilities would be valuable to your company…'*

> *'The manager of your Bristol branch, Pamela Bronson, suggested I contact you regarding the opening for a _____.'*

> *'I received your name from Henry Charles, the branch manager of the XYZ Bank last week, and he suggested I contact you. In case the CV he forwarded is delayed in the mail, I enclose another.'*

> *'Arthur Gold, your office manager and my neighbour, thought I should contact you about the upcoming opening in your accounting department.'*

2 Tell them why you are writing:

> *'It's time for me to make a move; my job just got sent to Mumbai, India, and I'm hoping you can help me with a new sense of direction.'*

3 Do not talk about your ideal job. This only narrows the opportunities people will tell you about. Instead, just let contacts know your qualifications/experience and the job title you are most likely to work under. Don't let ego cost you a valuable job lead.

4 Ask for advice and guidance:

> *'Who do you think are the developing companies in our industry today?'*

> *'Could you take a look at my CV for me? I really need an objective opinion and I've always respected your viewpoint.'*

5 Never ask directly, 'Do you have a job?' 'Can you hire me?' or 'Can your company hire me?' Instead, ask to talk on the telephone for a few minutes. Then by all means ask for leads within specific target companies.

6 When you do get help, say thank you. If you get the help in conversation, follow it up in writing; the impression is indelible and it just might get you another lead.

The broadcast letter

The broadcast letter acts as a brief introduction of the skills you bring to the table and is designed to be sent without a CV. You can use it when:

- you don't have a relevant CV;

- your CV is inappropriate for the position;

- your CV isn't getting the results you want, and you want to try something different while you are renovating it.

To be effective, the information you use in a broadcast letter must be relevant to the specific needs of a job posting or be focused on the needs of this job as you have determined them from your CV's target job deconstruction exercises (more on this shortly). This is because the intent of the broadcast letter is to *replace* the CV as a means of introduction and to initiate conversation. Keep in mind that although a broadcast letter can get you into a telephone conversation with a potential employer, that employer is still likely to ask for a CV.

While I am not a big fan of broadcast letters, people have used them effectively, so you need to be aware of them. As they more or less require you have a name to send them to, my feeling is that, as a CV is going to be requested anyway, you should take the time to customize your CV properly. I don't advise using this kind of letter as the spearhead or sole thrust of your campaign, but you can use it as a stopgap measure when you are renovating an ineffective CV or otherwise regrouping.

Networking letter (computer and information systems manager)

This letter was sent to follow up a meeting with a medical school dean.

DAVID KENT

1 Any Street • Anytown AA1 1AA
12345 678901 • dkent@alohanet.com

14 January 20–

John Jones, MD
Dean, School of Medicine
University of Hawaii
111 Any Avenue
Honolulu, Hawaii 96822

Dear Dr Jones,

Perhaps you remember our chance meeting at the Bio Asia-Pacific Conference at the Sheraton Waikiki on 18 and 19 August 20–. In our brief conversation, I shared with you the idea of using Web Development as an administrative tool. You expressed interest in the possibility of implementing such a system within the School of Medicine.

May I suggest a formal meeting to explore the idea?

I have some exciting and creative ideas, which may encourage you to take the next step towards realizing the positive impact a content management system would have in the School of Medicine. This would also be a great opportunity for us to discuss your goals and how an administrative intranet would help you reach them in a more timely and cost-effective manner.

In addition, there has recently been spirited discussion within the IT community on the topic of organizational continuity and its potential vulnerability due to advances in technology. I think you'll find the specific strategies I have to share with you worthy of consideration.

If you recall, my background is in Web Planning and Development, with specific skills in developing administrative intranets and public websites, and designing web-based software to address the internal and external reporting needs of organizations.

Enclosed is my CV attesting to my experience and specialities. I will contact you within the next few days to discuss the possibility of meeting with you.

Yours sincerely,

David Kent

David Kent
Computer and Information Systems Manager

Enclosure: CV

Broadcast letter

JANE SWIFT
1 Any Street, Anytown, AA1 1AA
12345 678901

2 October 20–

Dear Recipient's Name,

For the past seven years I have pursued an increasingly successful career in the sales profession. Among my accomplishments I include:

SALES
As a regional representative, I contributed £1,500,000, or 16 per cent, of my company's annual sales. I am driven by achievement.

MARKETING
My marketing skills (based on a BA in marketing) enabled me to increase sales by 25 per cent in my economically stressed territory, at a time when colleagues were striving to maintain flat sales. Repeat business reached an all-time high. I am persistent and pay attention to detail.

PROJECT MANAGEMENT
Following the above successes, my regional model was adopted by the company. I trained and provided project supervision to the entire sales force. The following year, company sales showed a sales increase 12 per cent above projections. I am a committed team player, motivated by the group's overall success.

The above was based on my firmly held zero price-discounting philosophy. I don't cut margins to make a sale. It is difficult to summarize my work in a letter. The only way I can imagine providing you with the opportunity to examine my credentials is for us to talk to each other. I look forward to hearing from you. Please call me at _____.

Yours sincerely,

Jane Swift

Jane Swift

Know the job, know your customer

Think of potential employers as your customers. When you listen to what your customers are saying, you will find that they will tell you exactly what they want to buy! Understanding what is important to your customer – the employer – helps you to understand what that customer wants to buy and what you need to sell.

If your job is in sales, marketing, marketing communications, or in any way close to bringing in revenue for your employer, you will understand the importance of 'getting inside your customer's head' to find out what is important to them, because this allows you to sell the product or service based on the customer's needs. Knowing what a customer wants to buy makes it much easier to customize your message to meet their needs.

All the insights you need to write a good cover letter are already available to you in job ads. *All you need to do is learn how to translate it into usable information*, which is what we are going to do now.

On the next couple of pages is a simple exercise called Target Job Deconstructions. *Do not skip this exercise – it can make an enormous difference to this job search and to your entire future career development*. It will tell you precisely how to prioritize the information you offer employers, give you examples for your letters, and a new way of understanding what it is you actually get paid for. The exercise will also tell you the topics you are most likely to be asked about at interviews and prepare you with suggestions for answers to those questions.

The exercise is geared towards:

- determining the precise requirements of the job you want;

- matching your skills to those requirements;

- identifying the story you need to tell in your cover letter and CV to highlight the match between your skills and those requirements.

The target job deconstruction

The most difficult part of any letter is knowing what to say and how to say it, but this approach ensures that the topics your letter addresses are going to be of the highest relevance to your customers and the words you should use will have greatest likelihood of resonating with the reader.

Step 1. Collect six job ads or online postings for jobs you are best qualified to do and jobs you would enjoy. If you are interested in more than one job you must prioritize them.

Step 2. Create a new document and title it 'TJD for _____ (your chosen target job title)'.

Step 3. Start with a first subhead reading 'Target job titles'. Then copy and paste in all the variations from your samples. Looking at the result, you will be able to say, 'When employers are hiring people like this, they tend to describe the job title with these words.' From this you can come up with a generic Target Job Title to use in your cover letters (and as a target job title for your CV) that is likely to have the widest response.

Step 4. Add a second subhead to the TJD: 'Skills/Responsibilities/ Requirements/Competencies, etc.'

Step 5. Look through the job postings (it might be easier to print them out and spread them across your desk). You are looking for a requirement that is common to all of your job postings. When you find both the requirement and the most complete description of it, copy and paste it into your document beneath the second subhead (with a 6 beside it, signifying it is common to all six of your samples).

Underneath, add any additional words and phrases used in the other job postings to describe this same area. Repeat this exercise for any other requirements common to all six of your job postings.

Step 6. Repeat the exercise but now consider requirements common to five of the jobs, then four, and so on, all the way down to those requirements mentioned in only one job ad.

You now have something unique: a template for how employers prioritize and express their needs when they hire someone like you.

Step 7. At their most elemental level, all jobs are the same – they all focus on problem identification, avoidance and solution. No matter what your job title is, you are being paid to prevent problems occurring whenever possible within your areas of responsibility and to solve them whenever they do crop up.

Imagine yourself, for a moment, as a manager looking at a cover letter and accompanying CV. Is this exactly the person you are looking for – someone who recognizes and knows how to handle the challenges of the job? Of course it is. When you as a job seeker register the underlying problem-solving nature of your target job, you gain a valuable insight into the mind of every recruiter, interviewer and manager you are ever going to meet.

Step 8. Now go back to your TJD and start with that first requirement, the one common to all six job postings. Note the problems you will typically need to identify, solve and/or prevent in the course of a normal workday as you deliver on this requirement of the job. Then list specific examples, big and small, of successful identification, prevention and/or solution to such problems that you've performed in the past.

Step 9. Repeat this with each of the TJD's other requirements, identifying the problems that come up in each aspect of the job and examples of how you deal with them. You'll want to include some of these examples in your cover letters. Others you'll use in your CV. Additional ones will provide you with the ammunition to answer all those interview questions that begin, 'Tell me about a time when…' and still others may appear in the follow-up letters after the interview.

Step 10. Look at each of the competencies/requirements you identified in steps 5 and 6, and for each one think of the *best* person you have ever seen doing this job and what made him or her stand out. Describe his or her performance, professional behaviour, interaction with others, and appearance.

This step has importance for today, tomorrow, and for your long-term success. This is the behavioural profile interviewers want to see in your cover letters, your CV, and at job interviews, and this is the person they would love to see showing up to work every day. In fact, this is the exact behavioural profile of the person who gets welcomed into the inner circle and gets the plum assignments, pay rises and promotions.

Repeat this behavioural identification exercise for each and every requirement listed in your TJD.

Step 11. Think of the *worst* person you have ever seen doing this job and answer for yourself what made that person stand out in such a negative way. Describe his or her performance, professional behaviours, interaction with others, and appearance. You are describing the person that no one wants to hire or work with; this valuable step gives you a behavioural profile for professional suicide.

Once you complete and review your TJD, you will have a clear idea of exactly the way all employers think about, prioritize and express their needs when they hire someone for the job you want. This tells you exactly the points to put in your cover letter that are most likely to get a positive response and prepares you in other ways for job interviews and for success in the job you ultimately choose as your next step.

4

Develop your professional identity

Competition is always fierce in a job search, so how you stand out from that competition is a big part of your success.

In this chapter, we'll talk about the issues and challenges of establishing a professional identity, and how to communicate that through your letters.

Written communication is a central component of your professional identity. It is easy for an interviewer to forget what someone is like, how they talk and what they say, but the written word has the capacity to bring you and your application back to life again in the interviewer's mind.

Your cover letter enables you to mark yourself out from the moment of introduction, and throughout the interview process when it presents a clear image of a unique, consummate professional. So, it helps to create a desirable professional identity that gives you focus and motivation and offers others an easy way to differentiate you from the crowd.

Identifying the components

A professional identity requires that you identify those skills and behaviours – your best professional qualities – that make you different and desirable. It's the capture and conscious positioning of those qualities in your letters, e-mails and on your CV that will make you stand out.

There are particular skills, values and behaviours that are admired by employers the world over. They are at the heart of all professional success because they can be applied in any job, at any level, in all professions.

I have broken this list of critical attributes into three sections:

1 Transferable skills

2 Professional values

3 Business values

Knowing its value to employers, when you identify one of these transferable skills, professional behaviours or core values as something you possess, make it part of your professional identity. When you identify a skill, behaviour or core value as something you need to develop, make it part of your ongoing personal development programme, because developing these attributes underlies your long-term survival and success.

Transferable skills

The National Association of Colleges and Employers (NACE), has defined seven transferable skills that every professional entering the workplace should develop:

Technical skills

Having technical skills means you know which tools are needed for a particular task and possess the know-how to use them productively and efficiently. These skills vary from profession to profession. Staying current with these skills is an integral part of your ongoing professional growth. Mentioning the course you just completed to upgrade your computer skills could be the perfect finish to a cover or follow-up letter.

Communication skills

Every professional job today requires communication skills; promotions and professional success are impossible without them.

The primary communication skills are:

- *Verbal skills:* What you say and how you say it.

- *Listening skills:* Listening to understand, rather than just waiting your turn to talk.

- *Writing skills:* Your ability to craft succinct, clear messages. Excellent written communication is essential for any professional career. It creates a lasting impression of who you are, and it's an important expression of your professional identity.

- *Technology communication skills:* Technology has changed the way we communicate and your ability to navigate the new communication media can and will have an impact on your professional success.

Teamworking skills

The professional world revolves around complex challenges and requires teams of people to provide solutions. This demands that you work efficiently with others who have different responsibilities, backgrounds, objectives and areas of expertise.

Critical thinking skills

Critical thinking, analytical, or problem-solving skills allow the successful professional to think through and clearly define a challenge and its desired solutions, and then evaluate and implement the best solution for that challenge from all available options.

Time management and organization skills

The ability to manage time and organize activities increases productivity. The people who do this are thought of as high achievers because they get so much done. In fact, these are just people who learned how to organize themselves and consequently work with more purpose.

Creativity

There's a difference between creativity and just having ideas. Creativity is developing those ideas with the strategic and tactical know-how that brings them to life. In a professional context, it is the generation of new ideas as they relate to a specific situation, challenge or goal. It is a skill that can be learned and applied to anything you do.

Leadership skills

Your job as a leader is to make your team function, so your teamwork skills give you the ability to pull your team together as a cohesive unit.

Your technical expertise, critical thinking and creativity skills help you to define the challenges and their solutions.

Your communication skills enable your team to understand its tasks and goals.

Your time management and organization skills enable you to create a practical blueprint for success and for your team to take ownership of the task and deliver the expected results.

Professional values

Successful professionals display these values in everything that they do. They'll open the doors of opportunity for you, too:

- *Motivation:* Employers realize that a motivated professional will do better on every assignment. Motivation expresses itself in a commitment to the job and the profession, an eagerness to learn and grow professionally, and a willingness to take the rough with the smooth.

- *Energy:* Motivation is invariably expressed by the energy someone demonstrates in his or her work, and is demonstrated by always giving that extra effort to get the job done and to get it done well.

- *Commitment:* These qualities include dedication to your profession and understanding the role it plays in the larger issues of company success. Knowing how your role contributes to the greater good gives you a strong sense of commitment.

- *Reliability:* Your dedication will also express itself in your reliability: Showing up is half the battle; the other half is your performance: not relying on anyone else to ensure the job is done.

- *Determination:* Determination is the quality of a resilient professional who doesn't get worn down or back off when a situation gets tough. It marks out the man or woman who chooses to be part of the solution rather than standing idly by and being part of the problem.

- *Pride:* Taking pride in yourself as a professional means always making sure you do your job to the best of your ability. It means paying attention to the details and to the time and cost constraints.

- *Integrity:* Integrity means taking responsibility for your actions, both good and bad, and it also means treating others, within and outside of the company, with respect at all times and in all situations. As a professional with integrity, your actions will always be in the ethical best interests of the company, and your decisions will never be based on whim or personal preference.

Business values

Companies have very limited interests: making money, saving money, and saving time. Developing business values that demonstrate sensitivity to the profit imperative of a business is the mark of a true professional.

These are all qualities that should be reflected in your professional identity, which in turn should appear in your job search letters and CV:

- *Productivity:* You should always work towards enhanced productivity through efficiencies of time, resources, money and effort. Most problems have two solutions, and the expensive one isn't always the best. Ideas of efficiency and economy engage the creative mind in ways that others would not consider.

- *Procedures:* You recognize the need for procedures and that they are implemented only after careful thought. You understand and always follow the chain of command and don't implement your own 'improved' procedures or organize others to do so.

Develop and apply these values in your professional life and you will become more credible, more visible and more successful as the result of having a developed professional identity.

However, that you possess these skills is one thing. That I know you possess them is another. Their inclusion in all your written communications should be an obvious step that we'll look at a little later in this chapter.

The examples of your skills and the impact of these values on your work can be used in all your job search letters to make positive statements about your suitability.

Identifying your competitive difference

Now that you have looked at the skills and values that mark successful professionals the world over, let's move on to pinpointing your competitive difference. This is another theme that must run throughout all your job search letters.

The people who hire you must be able to separate you from the other candidates. Your letters will reflect the qualities we discussed above, and this will help in that process, but we need more ammunition to make sure that you stand out. The following questions will help you identify the combination of factors that make you unique:

- What are the transferable skills, professional behaviours and business values that capture the essence of the professional you?

- What have you achieved with these qualities?

- What excites you most about your professional responsibilities?

- What are your biggest achievements in these areas?

- What gives you greatest satisfaction in the work you do?

- What value does this combination of skills, behaviours and achievements mean you bring to your employer?

- Make three one-sentence statements that capture the professional you.

- Take these three statements and rework them into one sentence. This is the essence of your competitive difference.

Weaving your professional identity into letters

These questions should help you to define your competitive difference and objectively sum up the professional you. These become the basis of the statements you use in your job search letters, CV and other written communications when it is necessary to talk about yourself.

Sometimes these will be bold statements and at other times an inference or subtle reference to make a point, but they all say, in effect, 'These are the benefits my presence will bring to your team and to your company.'

Your professional identity is communicated throughout your cover letter and CV, but especially in these statements.

Here is a statement from a pharmaceutical sales management professional:

I have attached my CV, where you will see a history of achievement with major pharmaceutical companies. I am well equipped to continue this success and would be honoured to join your team, where I believe I can outperform all prior achievements.

Implicit in this statement is a promise that this professional will repeat a history of achievement. She feels confident in doing so because her track record is underpinned with a clear sense of the skills this success is based upon. A couple of sentences in her cover letter demonstrate her value and make for a powerful presentation.

In another statement, a compelling message – 'I understand what is at the core of success in my job and I care about it' – is clearly emphasized:

With reference to your Customer Service posting on www.sales.com, are you looking for a customer service associate who treats every customer interaction as critical to the company's success?

Here are some more examples:

- I believe I can bring sound technical skills, strong business acumen, and real management skill to technical projects and personnel in a fast-paced environment.

- Five years' experience in a retail environment has taught me that customer service is the company's face to the world and I consequently treat every customer interaction as critical to financial success.

- Leadership by example and conscientious performance management underlies my department's consistent customer satisfaction ratings.

Job search letters are short documents with much to convey. Your cover letters and all your job search letters should support your professional identity by addressing the skills, behaviours and values that identify you as a professional.

5

Elements of a great cover letter

There is a fine line between pride in achievement and insufferable arrogance when writing about your experiences and who you are as a professional.

Now that you have a clearer idea of what makes you different, you're ready to reflect this in your cover letters and all the other types of letters you can use to make yourself stand out during the job hunt.

Differences between electronic and print cover letters

Today's workplace tends to demand 50 or more hours weekly from busy, multi-tasking professionals. Executives often base their decisions on whether to return a call or respond to an e-mail on the first few words of the message. If you can't cut to the chase, they think they shouldn't waste their time because of your communication inadequacies. *Your cover letter and CV, whether sent by e-mail or snail mail, competes for the attention of this audience.* The key is to construct a clear, well-ordered, compelling, *succinct* letter.

A cover letter is a collection of sequenced sentences organized around a single goal: to build a bridge between you and the recipient and get your CV read with serious attention. While it is likely that you will need to create more than one type of cover letter, start by creating one general letter first. You can then use this letter as a template to cut, paste and otherwise adapt to create other letters for different purposes. It should be brief and focus on the employer's needs.

Cover letter ingredients

Your letters will be most effective when you do each of the following seven things:

1 Address someone by name – whenever possible, find someone involved in the recruitment and selection cycle, ideally a hiring authority, as we noted – typically one to three management levels above your title.

2 Explain why you are writing, tailoring the letter to the reader/company as far as is practical.

3 Mention something you have discovered in common between you and the recipient, the job, or the company.

4 Include information relevant to the job you are seeking. As with the TJD you undertook earlier, this is possible even when you do not have a job posting.

5 Show concern, interest and pride in your work; the branding exercises from the last chapter will help you with this.

6 Maintain a balance between professionalism and friendliness.

7 Ask for the next step in the process clearly and without apology or arrogance.

Before discussing formatting, let's take a minute to talk in more detail about some of these issues.

What makes a cover letter work?

Your first step is to grab the reader's attention. Whenever possible, your letter should start with a personalized greeting. E-mail has increased our ease of communication and relaxed a number of letter writing rules, but you must always use a greeting/salutation to open your letter and set a professional tone. If you do not start your letter with a greeting you are immediately seen as someone who does not have a basic grasp of business communication. Because written communication is so important in today's workplace, no salutation can mean your letter is ignored.

That's why you want to open the letter by using a person's name, spelled correctly and using one of the following forms:

- Dear Mr Yate (standard);

- Hello, Mr Yate (more casual but still OK; not as acceptable in the professions of law, medicine and education);

- Dear Martin Yate or Hello, Martin Yate (acceptable if you are an experienced professional, but not so much if you are at the entry level or in your first two or three years in the professional workplace).

Do not use first names (Hello, Martin or Dear Carole) when you haven't communicated with the reader before. First names are OK once you have spoken and are clearly on a first-name basis, when you are of a similar age and professional standing. If you are younger, even if you have been encouraged to use first names, only do so in person. When writing, use a more formal address. It is a sign of respect that is invariably appreciated.

Starting the letter

Everything you need to say must be short and to the point so that your copy never exceeds one page. At the same time, you want to find common ground with your reader and present yourself in the best way. Use the first paragraph to introduce yourself and establish your reason for writing.

Here are a few examples:

When you have a referral or prior frame of reference

First things first, Carole Mraz over at C-Soft asked me to say hello. You and I haven't spoken before but Carole thinks we might have an interesting conversation, especially if you anticipate the need for an industrious young marketing acolyte who comes equipped with a great education, two ears and one mouth, and a great desire to start at the bottom learning from an acknowledged master in the field.

Our mutual colleague, John Stanovich, felt my skills and abilities would be valuable to your company…

The manager of your Brighton office, Pamela Bronson, has suggested I contact you regarding the opening for a _____.

I received your name from Henry Charles, the branch manager of the ABC Bank, last week and he suggested I contact you. In case the CV he forwarded is delayed in the mail, I enclose another.

Arthur Gold, your office manager and my neighbour, thought I should contact you about the upcoming opening in your accounting department.

A colleague of mine, Diane Johnson, recommended your recruitment company to me as you recently assisted her in a strategic career move. I understand that your company specializes in the consumer products industry.

I met you briefly at the import/export symposium last _____ and your comments about productivity being pulled down by sloppy communications really resonated with me. As I am looking to harness my _____ years of logistics expertise to an organization with a major role in global distribution…

When you have no referral and no job posting

I have been researching the leading local companies in _____ , and the name of _____ Products keeps coming up as a top company. This confirmed an opinion I've developed over my three years as a committed distance-learning educator.

Right after my mentor mentioned _____ as one of the top companies in our industry, I saw you speak at the association meeting last year. I really resonated with your comments about productivity, and as I am looking to harness my _____ years of logistics expertise to a major player, I felt this was the right time to introduce myself.

I understand you are a manager who likes to gets things done, and who needs competent, focused, goal-orientated employees…

I'm focused on finding the right boss to bring out the best in a consistently top-producing _____ . I am a highly motivated producer who wants to make a contribution as part of the hard-driving team of the industry leader.

I thought the best way to demonstrate my drive and creativity was to deliver my CV in this priority mail envelope. I also sent it to you by e-mail and into your company CV bank, but sales is all about stacking the odds, and I knew you'd also appreciate a break from the computer screen.

I've been meaning to contact you ever since I attended/read/heard about _____ . It encouraged me to do a little research, which has convinced me that you are the kind of company I want to be associated with, and that I have the kind of analytical focus coupled with creative drive that can be successfully applied to your current projects.

I have been following the performance of your company in Mutual Funds Newsletter. With my experience working for one of your direct competitors in office support in the critical area of customer service I know I could make significant contributions… I am a detail-orientated problem solver and am used to working with different, often frustrated people.

Recently, I have been researching the local _____ industry. My search has been focused on looking for companies that are respected in the field and that prize a commitment to professional development. I am such an individual and you are clearly such a company. I bring sound technical skills, strong business acumen, and real management skills for complex technical projects in a fast-paced environment.

Although I am currently employed by one of your major competitors, I must admit that I was captivated by your company's mission statement when I visited your website.

Within the next few weeks, I will be moving from Glasgow to _____ . Having researched the companies in _____ , I know that you are the company I want to talk to because…

The state of the art in _____ changes so rapidly that it is tough for most professionals to keep up. The attached CV will demonstrate that I am an exception and eager to bring my experience as a _____ to bear for your company.

When you are responding to a job posting

Your job posting no. 23567 cited the need for drive and creativity. I thought a good way to demonstrate my drive and creativity was to deliver my CV in this priority mail envelope. Of course, I sent it to you by e-mail, but marketing communications is all about psychology and results… so I knew you'd get the message, appreciate the contrarian thinking, and enjoy a break from the computer screen.

I read your job posting on your company's website on 5th January and felt I had to respond…

Your online job posting regarding a _____ on _____.com caught my eye, and your company name caught my attention.

This e-mail, and my attached CV, is in response to your job posting on _____ .

I read your advertisement in the Daily Press on 6th October for a _____ and, after researching your company website, felt I had to write…

Reference job no. C/AA 5670. As you compare your requirements for a _____
with my attached CV, you will see that my entire background matches your requirements exactly.

This letter and attached CV are in response to your posting in _____ *.*

I was excited to see your opening for the accounting vacancy (job no. S9854) on careerbuilder.co.uk. As my attached CV demonstrates, the open position is a perfect match for my 15 years' payroll, general ledger, and accounts receivable experience.

While browsing the jobs database on monster.co.uk, I was intrigued by your Regional Sales Manager job posting.

Presenting yourself

If you haven't managed to build in the reason for writing into your opening as we see in some of the above examples, introduce it now and go on to identify something desirable about the professional you.

I am writing because…

My reason for contacting you…

… you may be interested to know…

If you are seeking a _____ *, you will be interested to know…*

I would like to talk to you about your need for _____ *and how I might be able to contribute to your department's goals.*

If you have an opening for someone in this area, you will see that my CV demonstrates a person of unusual dedication, efficiency and drive.

You then go on to define the kind of work you do with a brief statement and/or two to three statements that highlight your capabilities. With a short paragraph or a couple of bullet-points you might highlight one or two special contributions or achievements. These can include any qualifications, contributions and attributes that brand you as someone with talent and energy to offer.

You can also use this part of the letter if an aspect of a particular job opening is not addressed in your CV, and for some reason you don't have time to update it.

Or you can use the cover letter to emphasize a priority requirement from the posting.

In my CV you will find proof of my PR acumen including:

- *demonstrated track record of strategic communications and influential public relations;*

- *accomplished media relations and story placement, from* BBC World News *to* ZDNet;

- *team, account, budget, client and C-level executive management;*

- *client loyalty and satisfaction;*

- *knowledge of high-tech industry and players;*

- *new business success;*

- *self-motivated team player.*

Although I am currently employed by one of your competitors, I have kept my eye open for an opportunity to join your organization. Over the past year I have:

- *built a sales force of seven reps, reduced turnover, and increased individual productivity an average of 14 per cent;*

- *implemented a customer service plan that successfully reduced client turnover 18 per cent;*

- *initiated warranty tracking, increasing upselling by 7 per cent;*

- *increased revenue by £4.3 million.*

As a Marketing Director with 12 years' experience in consumer products, I have:

- *doubled revenues in just 18 months;*

- *introduced a new product that captured a 38 per cent market share;*

- *successfully managed a £5 million ad budget.*

I have an economics background from Cambridge and employ cutting-edge quantitative analysis strategies to approach cyclical fluctuations. This has enabled me to anticipate all major peaks and valleys consistently during the last 12 years.

I noticed from your posting that training experience in a distance-learning environment would be a plus. You will see from my enclosed CV that I have five years' experience writing and producing sales and management training materials in new media.

You are looking for a database administrator with experience of intranet implementation and management. As my attached CV demonstrates, I have done that type of work for six years with a regional organization on a platform of 15,000 users.

Desk technology upgrades:

- *responsible for hardware and peripheral selection;*

- *coordinated installation of workstations;*

- *trained users.*

Full upgrade achieved under budget and within deadline. Savings to company: £25,000.

You want the reader to move from your letter to the CV already primed with the feeling that you can do this job; the reference to a job's key requirement does just that. Since you want the reader to move quickly to your CV, brevity is important. Leave your reader wanting more; the letter doesn't sell you – that's the CV's job – but it should position you for serious consideration. Whet the reader's appetite, no more.

Make it clear to the reader that you want to talk

Explain when, where and how you can be contacted. You can also be proactive, by telling the reader that you intend to follow up at a certain point in time if contact has not been established by then. Just as you worked to create a strong opening, make sure your closing carries the same conviction. It is the reader's last personal impression of you, so make it strong, make it tight, and make it obvious that you are serious about entering into meaningful conversation.

Useful phrases include:

It would be a pleasure to give you more information about my qualifications and experience…

I welcome the opportunity to discuss your specific projects and explore the possibility of joining your team.

I look forward to discussing our mutual interests further…

I prefer not to use my employer's time taking personal calls at work, instead you reach me on _____ .

I will be in your area around the 20th, and will call you prior to that date. I would like to arrange…

I have attached my CV for your review and will call you in the next couple of days to discuss any openings for which your firm is currently conducting searches.

I hope to speak with you further, and will call the week of _____ to follow up.

The chance to meet you would be a privilege and a pleasure, so to this end I shall call you on _____ .

I look forward to speaking to you further, and will call in the next few days to see when our schedules will permit a face-to-face meeting.

May I suggest a personal meeting where you can have the opportunity to examine the person behind the CV?

My credentials and achievements are a matter of record that I hope you will examine in depth when we meet. You can reach me at _____ .

I look forward to discussing any of the ways you feel my background and skills would benefit [name of organization]. I look forward to hearing from you.

CVs help you sort out the probables from the possibles, but they are no way to judge the calibre of an individual. I would like to meet you and demonstrate that I have the professional personality that makes for a successful _____ .

I expect to be in your area on Tuesday and Wednesday of next week, and wonder which day would be best for you. I will call to determine. In the meantime, I would appreciate you treating my application as confidential, since I am currently employed.

With my training and hands-on experience, I know I can contribute to _____ , and want to talk to you about it in person. When may we meet?

After reading my CV, you will know something about my background. Yet you will still need to determine whether I am the one to help you with current problems and challenges. I would like an interview to discuss my ability to make meaningful contributions to your department's goals.

You can reach me at [home/alternate no.] to arrange an interview. I know that the investment of your time in meeting with me will be repaid amply.

Thank you for your time and consideration; I hope to hear from you shortly.

May I call you for an interview in the next few days?

A brief phone call will establish whether or not we have mutual interest. Recognizing the demands of your schedule, I will make that call before lunch on Tuesday.

Some people feel it is powerful in the closing to state a date – 'I'll call you on Friday if we don't speak before' – or a date and time – 'I'll call you on Friday morning at 10 am if we don't speak before' when they will follow up with a phone call. The logic is that you demonstrate that your intent is serious, that you are organized, and that you plan your time effectively, all of which are desirable behavioural traits and support the brand of a goal-oriented and consummate professional.

A complete idiot in my profession once said that an employer would be offended by being 'forced' to sit and await this call. In over 30 years of involvement in the hiring process, as a headhunter, as a hiring manager, as an HR executive and as a writer on these issues who speaks to executives all over the world, I have never met anyone who felt constrained to wait by the phone for such a call. What sometimes does get noticed, though, is the person who doesn't follow through on commitments as promised. Therefore, if you use this approach, keep your promise: it's part of your professionalism.

Now that you have a frame of reference for the factors that affect cover letters and any other job search letters, let's move on to the nuts and bolts of making them work.

> Later in the book you'll find five types of cover letters, plus follow-up letters; networking letters; thank you letters; resurrection letters; and acceptance, rejection, and resignation letters.

A question of money

Recruitment advertisements sometimes request salary information, either current salary, salary requirements or salary history. Over the years this issue has taken far more of people's attention than it deserves.

Recruiters and employers ask about your salary for two principal reasons:

1 *Because all jobs have approved salary ranges* and no matter what your skills, it is hard to win an exception to an approved salary range.

2 *Because it tells them about your salary trajectory*, the offer you are likely to accept and the pay rises you are used to.

There are other considerations as well: interviews take precious time, and managers are reluctant to waste it on candidates who could never be hired because of their salary needs.

If there is an exception, it is when you are in a hot job within an in-demand professional area or you have a unique skill set that gives you a competitive edge.

In a falling economy when money is tighter and they have more options, it is known as a buyer's market and employers have far less incentive to negotiate outside the approved salary.

Writing that your salary is 'negotiable', annoys HR people: they already know salary is negotiable, and the reply doesn't answer the question they need answered.

With an in-demand job in a good economy, 'negotiable' is rarely grounds for refusing to talk to a candidate, but in a buyer's market 'negotiable' might not always have the desired result.

Given this understanding, if you have the skills and you are in the approved range you'll get an interview. If you aren't... well, then your energies are probably better invested in finding other opportunities, but make the pitch anyway. You have nothing to lose.

When your salary requirements are requested, don't restrict yourself to one figure; instead, give yourself a range. All job openings have an approved salary range so this dramatically improves your chances of 'fitting into' the salary range that is authorized for every position.

If you are asked about your current salary and choose to answer, be honest. This isn't something you can ever fudge. It can and does get verified, and any discrepancies can result in you being dismissed; such an event will dog your career for years. Here is one way to address the topic of money in your cover letter. You will find other examples later in the book.

Depending on the job and the professional development environment, my salary requirements are in the £_____ to £_____ range.

Address this issue in the cover letter or in a document attached to the cover letter not in the CV itself.

Here is an example of a salary history attachment.

Calvin Tompkins

1 Any Street, Anytown AA1 1AA

Home 12345 678901 • Mobile 1098765 4321 • sharplogistics@gmail.com

Salary History

XYZ Avionics, Kings Weston – 2008 to 2010

Chief Operations Officer / Aviation Training School Officer in Charge

Salary – £55,207

ABC Aviation, Leicester – 2006 to 2008

Aircraft Maintenance Chief – General Operations Manager / Plant Manager

Starting Salary – £44,484 / Ending Salary – £50,500

XYZ Systems, Birmingham – 2002 to 2006

Plant Manager / Senior Operations Manager

Starting Salary – £40,507 / Ending Salary – £44,200

ABC Engineering – 1998 to 2002

Recruitment Manager

Starting Salary – £35,545 / Ending Salary – £42,500

Contact information

With e-mail, your return address is built into your communication and you can add a phone number beneath your signature. A printed letter should include address, telephone number and e-mail address. Once you have decided on a primary contact number for your job hunt, you must ensure that it will be answered *at all times*. There is no point in mounting a job search campaign if prospective employers can never reach you. Your telephone company offers you voice mail; use it and keep the message businesslike and, once recorded, replay it and listen carefully to the message for clarity, tone of voice, and recording quality. Does it present you as a clear-spoken, confident professional, and does it reflect the professional brand you are trying to create?

In your cover letter, you should always list your e-mail address immediately beneath your telephone number, as initial contact is often by e-mail. Never use your company telephone or e-mail for any job search activities, ever.

If you're sending out your cover letters by e-mail with CV attachments, make sure your e-mail address in your CV is hyperlinked (it appears in another colour, usually blue). That way, recruiters can send an e-mail back to you with one click of the mouse directly from your CV. Remember, it's all about making it *easy* for hiring managers to contact you. The less work you make them do, the better your chances of success.

Assembling your job search letter

There are six steps to organizing the building blocks of your cover letter into a coherent, effective whole.

Step one: identify your target job

Your job search – and the CV and letters that go with it – will be incalculably more productive if you begin by clearly defining a target job that you can land and in which you can be successful. Start by identifying this target job title.

Step two: research the target job

Any evaluation of your background must begin with an understanding of what potential employers will be looking for when they come to your cover letter and CV. Collect 6 job postings that carry this target job title. Once you have a selection, deconstruct them as described in the Target Job Deconstruction process.

Step three: review your recent work history

Once you know what your readers are looking for and therefore will respond to, it is time to start working through your work history. Knowing what your customers want to buy (as revealed in the Target Job Deconstruction) and how to illustrate your abilities to deliver on their needs is part of this story. So consider, for example, the following elements:

A Current or last employer

Identify your current or most recent employer by name and location, and follow it with a brief description (five or six words) of the company's business/products/services.

B Duties: Make a prioritized list of the duties/responsibilities/deliverables in this position.

C Skills: What special skills or knowledge did you need to perform each of these tasks well? Which transferable skills and professional values helped you execute each of these tasks successfully?

- What educational background and/or credentials helped prepare you for these responsibilities?

- For each area of responsibility consider the daily problems that arise and also major crises. Recall the analytical processes, subsequent actions, the transferable skills and successful solutions you implemented to achieve a successful outcome. There is a four-step technique you will find useful here called PSRV:

P. Identify the *project* and the problem it represented, both from a company perspective and from the point of view of your execution of duties.

S. Identify your *solution* to the challenge and the process you implemented to deliver the solution.

R. What was the *result* of your approach and actions?

V. Finally, what was the *value* to you, the department, and the company? If you can, define this in terms of meaningful contribution: time saved, money saved, or money earned. This is not always possible, but it is very powerful whenever you can employ it.

Step four: consider transferable skills and professional values used

Which transferable skills and professional values helped you succeed with this particular task? Come up with examples of how you used each particular skill in the execution of each of your major duties at this job. The examples you generate can be used in your CV, in your cover letters and as illustrative answers to questions at interviews.

Step five: add your previous work history

Now repeat Steps 3 (the problem solving aspect of your job) and 4 (how you used your transferable skills and professional values with each of your previous jobs). Do not skimp on this process. Everything you write may not go into the final version of your first cover letter, but you'll be able to use the information in another letter, in your CV, or in response to an interview question. What you are doing is identifying the building blocks of what it takes to be successful in your profession, and the information you need at your fingertips to explain what you do objectively. The ultimate pay-off is more and better job offers and a more successful career.

Step six: compile compliments

Looking at each of your major areas of responsibility throughout your work history, write down any positive verbal or written commentary others have made on your performance. As you will see in some of the sample letters, words about you that come from someone else often have a much greater impact than any description you could come up with yourself.

Now, these compliments don't always happen that often, and then all too often you sometimes push the accolades away. That's OK – lots of people do – but from now on you will make a point of capturing them for use in the future.

> How did you work productively with co-workers, subordinates, and management? What different levels of people do you have to interact with to achieve your job's goals? What have you learned about productivity and communication from these experiences, and what does this say about you?

Create punchy sentences

Any letter is only as good as the individual sentences that carry the message. Your goal is to communicate an energizing message and entice the reader to action. Concise, punchy sentences grab attention.

Verbs always help energize a sentence and give it that short, cut-to-the-chase feel. For example, one professional – with a number of years at the same law firm in a clerical position – had written:

I learned to manage a computerized database.

Sounds pretty ordinary, right? Well, after looking at her job as an ongoing problem-solving exercise, certain exciting facts emerged. By using verbs and an awareness of employer interests as they relate to her target job, this sentence was charged up and given more punch. Not only that, but for the first time the writer fully understood the value of her contributions, which greatly enhanced her self-confidence for interviews:

I analysed and determined need for comprehensive upgrade of database, archival and retrieval systems. I was responsible for selection and installation of 'cloud-based' archival systems. Company-wide archival system upgrade completed in one year.

Notice how the verbs show that things happened when she was around the office and put flesh on the bones of that initial bare statement. Such action verbs and phrases add an air of direction, efficiency and accomplishment to every cover letter. Succinctly, they tell the reader *what* you did and *how well* you did it.

As you recall information that will contribute to your cover letter, rewrite key phrases to see if you can give them more depth with the use of action verbs. While a cover letter is typically one page, or one screen, don't worry about the length just now. The process you go through helps you think through exactly what it is you have to offer and also creates the language and ideas you will use to explain yourself during an interview.

Varying sentence structure

As noted in the previous section, your letters will be most effective when they are constructed with short, punchy sentences. As a rule, try keeping your sentences under about 25 words; a good average is around 15. If your sentence is longer than the 25-word mark, change it. Either shorten it through restructuring, use semicolons to save space instead of all the words necessary to start a whole new sentence, or make two sentences out of one. At the same time, you will want to avoid choppiness, so vary the length of sentences when you can.

You can also start with a short phrase ending in a colon:

- followed by bullet-points of information;

- each one supporting the original phrase.

These techniques are designed to enliven the reading process for readers, who always have too much to read and too little time. Here's how we can edit and rewrite the last example.

Analysed and determined need for comprehensive upgrade of database, archival and retrieval systems:

- *Responsible for software selection and system-wide compatibility.*

- *Responsible for selection and installation of 'cloud-based' archival systems.*

- *Trained users from manager to administrators.*

- *Achieved full upgrade, integration and compliance in six months. Manager stated, 'You brought us out of the dark ages, and neither you nor the firm missed a beat!'*

K.I.S.S. (keep it simple, stupid)

Persuading your readers to take action is challenging because many people in different companies and with different agendas see your letters and make judgements based on those agendas. This means you must keep industry jargon to a reasonable level (especially in the initial contact letters – covers, broadcast and the like); the rule of thumb is to use only the jargon and acronyms used in the advertisement. Some readers will understand the intricacies and technicalities of your profession, but many more will not.

Within your short paragraphs and short sentences, beware of name dropping and acronyms, such as 'I worked for Dr A Witherspoon in Sys. Gen. SNA 2.31.' Statements like these can be too restricted to have meaning outside the small circle of specialists to whom they speak. Unless you work in a highly technical field, and are sending the letter and CV to someone by name and title that you know will understand the importance of your technical language, you should use technical phrases with discretion.

You want your letters to have the widest possible appeal, yet they need to remain personal in tone, so they don't sound like they're from Publishers Clearing House. You are trying to capture the essence of the professional you in just a few brief paragraphs. Short words in short sentences help make short, gripping paragraphs – good for short attention spans!

Voice and tense

The voice you use for different letters depends on a few important factors:

- getting a lot said in a small space;

- packaging your skills and credentials for the target job;

- being factual;

- capturing the essence and personality of the professional you.

There is considerable disagreement among the 'experts' about the best voice, and each option has both champions and detractors. The most important point is that whichever voice you use in your letters, you must be consistent throughout that letter.

Sentences can be truncated (up to a point), by omitting pronouns such as *I, you, he, she, they*:

Analysed and determined need for comprehensive upgrade of database…

In fact, many authorities recommend dropping pronouns as a technique that both saves space and allows you to brag about yourself without seeming boastful. It gives the impression of another party writing about you. Some feel that to use the personal pronoun – *'I analysed and determined need for comprehensive upgrade of database…'* – is naive, unprofessional, and smacks of boasting. However, still others recommend that you write in the first person because it makes you sound more human.

In short, there are no hard-and-fast rules – they can all work, given the many unique circumstances you will face in any given job search. It is common in CVs to cut out personal pronouns, but given the more personal nature of a letter, there is a danger of the message sounding too choppy without pronouns. Use whatever style works best for you and for the particular letter you are writing. If you do use the personal pronoun, try not to use it in every sentence; it gets a little monotonous, and it can make you sound like an egomaniac. The mental focus should be not on 'I' but on 'you', the person with whom you are communicating.

A nice variation is to use a first-person voice throughout the letter and then a final few words in the third person. Make sure these final words appear in the form of an attributed quote, as an insight to your value:

> *Manager stated, 'You brought us out of the dark ages, and neither you nor the firm missed a beat!'*

Don't confuse professionalism in your job search letters with stuffy formality. The most effective tone is one that mixes the conversational and the formal, just as we do in our offices and on our jobs. The only overriding rule is to make the letter readable so that the reader can see a human being and a professional shining through the page.

Length

As I indicated earlier, the standard length for a cover letter is usually one page, or the equivalent length for e-mails; typically this is as much as you can see on your screen without scrolling. Subsequent letters stemming from verbal communications – whether over the telephone or face-to-face – should also strive to keep to the one-page rule, but can run to two pages if the complexity of content demands it.

With conscientious editing over a couple of days, that two-page letter can usually be reduced to one page without losing any of the content, and at the same time it will probably pack more punch. As my editor always says, 'If in doubt, cut it out.'

Having said this, I should acknowledge that all rules are made to be broken. Occasionally a two-page letter might be required, generally in one of the following instances:

1   You are at a level, or your job is of such technical complexity, that you cannot edit down to one page without using a font size that is all but unreadable.

2   You have been contacted directly by an employer about a specific position and have been asked to present information for a specific opportunity.

3   An executive recruiter who is representing you decides that the exigencies of a particular situation warrant a dossier of such length. (Often such a letter and CV will be prepared exclusively by – or with considerable input from – the recruiter.)

You'll find that thinking too much about length considerations will hamper the writing process. Think instead of the story you have to tell, and then layer fact upon fact until your tale is told. Use your words and the key phrases from this book to craft the message of your choice. When *that* is done you can go back and ruthlessly cut it to the bone.

Ask yourself these questions:

- Can I cut out any paragraphs?

- Can I cut out any sentences?

- How can I reduce the word count of the longer sentences?

- Where have I repeated myself?

Whenever you can, cut something out – leave nothing but facts and action verbs! If at the end you find too much has been cut, you'll have the additional pleasure of reinstating your prose.

7

How to polish and edit your letters for maximum impact

Any job search letter is only as good as the individual sentences that carry your message. The most grammatically correct sentences in the world won't necessarily get you interviews, because they can read as though every breath of life has been squeezed out of them. Your goal is to communicate an energizing message and entice the reader to action.

A cover letter typically consists of 3–5 carefully constructed paragraphs. That's plenty of space to get your message across – and a second page simply won't get read.

Just as you would limit a printed cover letter to one page, you should try to keep an e-mail cover letter to one screen: that's as compact as possible. If you cannot get your entire letter into one screen view, at least make an effort to be certain that the meat of your pitch is on that first full screen.

The amount of e-mail traffic is growing exponentially, so hit your main points quickly and with clarity or lose your reader's attention. A good subject line grabs attention, but if the first two sentences don't succinctly state your purpose and maintain that initial attention, the reader has little reason for wasting any more precious time on the rest of your message.

Your professional business correspondence should demonstrate your written communication skills with powerful messaging that omits extraneous information and delivers the message in a format that is a model of clarity: easily accessible to both the eye and the mind.

Readability

Whether delivered by e-mail or in an envelope, your CV and letter will typically arrive on a reader's desktop when he or she has a dozen other priorities. You can expect your letter to get *a maximum five-second scan to see if it is worth reading*; this will cover the subject line/opening sentence, spelling of the recipient's name and general readability. If it passes the scan test, you probably have *30 seconds* to make your point, and that's assuming your letter cuts to the chase and addresses the reader's needs.

Mistakes to avoid

Letters that never get read have four things in common:

- They have too much information crammed into the space and are difficult to read – clearly the customer doesn't come first.

- The layout is unorganized, illogical and uneven; it looks shoddy and slapdash – and no one wants an employee like that.

- The recipient's name is misspelled – that's disrespectful.

- The letter contains typos – not acceptable in the age of spell-checkers.

Get your head into clear communication mode

Your CV and cover letters will always compete for the attention of a consistently distracted audience. The good news is that while your cover letters have a difficult job to do, if you apply just a few simple tactics, you can create one that dramatically increases the impact of your accompanying CV.

Advertising copywriters, with their ability to entertain and sell us stuff in a 30-second commercial, are arguably society's most effective communicators. They all share one common approach to their work: they get inside, and stay inside, the customer's head throughout the writing process. They focus on what features their product possesses and which benefits are most likely to appeal to the customer.

With your Target Job Deconstruction in hand, you know with considerable accuracy what your customer wants to hear about. You know what features and benefits you have to offer and with this self-knowledge, you have everything you need to polish the draft letter you have just created.

How long should it be?

We've been here before, and the answer's still the same. Long enough to make your point and not a word longer. The standard length for a cover letter is usually one page (about 300 words); with an e-mail, the equivalent is typically as much as you can see on your screen without scrolling. They can also be much shorter. Here is a cover letter that gets to the point in 71 words:

> *Your colleague, Bill Jacobson, suggested that I send you my CV. He mentioned that your department is looking for a database administrator with experience in intranet implementation and management. As my attached CV demonstrates, I have done that type of work for six years with a regional organization on a platform of 15,000 users. I welcome the opportunity to discuss your specific projects and explore the possibility of joining your team.*

With conscientious editing (spread over a couple of days to give you an objective distance), you can get any letter down to 300 words. The result will pack more punch.

Avoid acronyms and professional slang

Every profession has its acronyms and professional slang/jargon, but there will be people in the recruitment and selection cycle who don't get it all. The acronyms and jargon have their place in your CV, but try to keep them under control in your letters.

The rule of thumb is that if it is mentioned in the job postings you can use it. If not, find another way of saying it.

Give action to your statements with verbs

The focus of your letter echoes the keywords identified in your TJD: the keywords found in the job postings. These words are invariably nouns, but simply listing them doesn't make for an interesting story. Use verbs that show you in action.

- Responsible for all Accounts Payable

- Reduced Accounts Payable by…

- Streamlined Accounts Payable by…

- Managed all Accounts Payable…

Verbs always help energize a sentence and give it that short, cut-to-the-chase feel.

Verbs show you in action: they give the reader a point of view, a way to see you. Verbs are an important part of creating your professional brand because they impart an air of direction, efficiency and accomplishment to your written communications. Succinctly, they tell the reader *what* you did and *how well* you did it and by implication anticipate you performing to the same standards when on the letter reader's payroll.

To help you in the process, here are more than 175 action verbs you can use. This list is just a beginning. Just about every word-processing program has a thesaurus; you can type any one of these words into one and get more choices for each entry.

accomplished	calculated	cut	executed	initiated
achieved	catalogued	decreased	expanded	innovated
acted	chaired	delegated	expedited	inspected
adapted	clarified	demonstrated	explained	installed
addressed	classified	designed	extracted	instigated
administered	coached	developed	fabricated	instilled
advanced	collected	devised	facilitated	instituted
advised	compiled	diagnosed	familiarized	instructed
allocated	completed	directed	fashioned	integrated
analysed	composed	dispatched	focused	interpreted
appraised	computed	distinguished	forecast	interviewed
approved	conceptualized	diversified	formulated	introduced
arranged	conducted	drafted	founded	invented
assembled	consolidated	edited	generated	launched
assigned	contained	educated	guided	lectured
assisted	contracted	eliminated	headed	led
attained	contributed	enabled	identified	maintained
audited	controlled	encouraged	illustrated	managed
authored	coordinated	engineered	implemented	marketed
automated	corresponded	enlisted	improved	mediated
balanced	counselled	established	increased	moderated
budgeted	created	evaluated	influenced	monitored
built	critiqued	examined	informed	motivated

negotiated	produced	referred	schooled	systematized
operated	programmed	regulated	screened	tabulated
organized	projected	rehabilitated	set	taught
originated	promoted	remodelled	shaped	trained
overhauled	provided	repaired	solidified	translated
oversaw	publicized	represented	solved	travelled
performed	published	researched	specified	trimmed
persuaded	purchased	restored	stimulated	upgraded
planned	recommended	restructured	streamlined	validated
prepared	reconciled	retrieved	strengthened	worked
presented	recorded	revitalized	summarized	wrote
prioritized	recruited	saved	supervised	
processed	reduced	scheduled	surveyed	

Vary sentence length

As noted, your letters will be most effective when they are constructed with short, punchy sentences. Try keeping your sentences under about 25 words; a good average is around 15 to 20. If your sentence is longer than the 25-word mark, either shorten it through restructuring, or make two sentences out of one. You can also start with a short phrase ending in a colon:

- Followed by bullet-points of information.

- Each bullet supporting the original phrase. Doing this enlivens the reading experience, keeping the reader engaged.

- When possible, substitute short words for long words, and one word where previously there were two.

Short sentences should be part of short paragraphs creating plenty of white space so that reading is easy on the eye. Everything you need to say is said succinctly so that your letter never exceeds one page.

Fonts

The font you choose has a big impact on the readability of your work. Stay away from script-like fonts, and use only those accepted as suitable for professional communication. Script may be more visually appealing, but the goal is accessibility for a reader who is ploughing through stacks of CVs when he or she gets your message.

The font(s) you choose must be used in a size legible for managers. Anyone who has been staring at computer screens for 10 or more years is likely to suffer from eyestrain and have problems with 10-point fonts; 11- or 12-point fonts are recommended.

Your branding message stays strong and consistent by using the same font choices (and paper) for your letters as you use for your CV.

The font you used for contact information and headlines in your CV is the same font you will use for your letterhead. The font you chose for your CV's body copy is the same as you will use for the message in your letters.

Good for Headlines/Your Contact Information/Signature

Arial
Times
Century Gothic
Verdana
Gill Sans
Lucida Sans

Good for Body Copy of Your Letters

Bodoni
Garamond
Georgia
Goudy Old Style

Note: copy written in all capital letters, in any font, is harder to read.

How to brighten the page

Once you decide on a font, *stick with it*. Apart from headlines and contact information, more than one font on a page can look confusing. You can do plenty to liven up the visual impact of the page within the variations of the font you have chosen.

All the recommended fonts come in regular, bold, italic, underlined, and bold italic, so you can vary the impact of key words with *italics*, <u>underlined phrases</u>, and **boldface** for additional emphasis. For example, when you are sending a cover letter and CV in response to an internet job posting or recruitment advertisement, you can bold or italicize those words used by the employer in the ad, emphasizing your match to their needs.

You should stay away from exclamation points and emoticons. In the samples section you will find little variation on the font choice beyond an occasionally italicized word or word in bold. In the end, it's your judgement call. Just don't overdo the typographic pyrotechnics.

> Another no-no is the use of clip art to brighten the page. Those little quill pens and scrolls may look nifty to you, but they look amateurish to the rest of the world.

E-mail considerations

Do not include your e-mail address, because this, along with the date and time of your communication are entered automatically. If you are attaching a CV, your address will be seen there.

Subject line

Provide a revealing and concise subject line. It should allow the receiver to know immediately who you are and what you want.

The use of a powerful subject line can mean the difference between someone opening your e-mail or hitting the delete key. Think of a magazine or newspaper with headlines designed to grab the reader and draw him or her into the story. With an e-mail your subject line is your headline; it draws the reader into your e-mail. Your subject line needs to be intriguing and it also needs to be professional.

Do not use a subject line that states the obvious, like 'CV' or 'Jim Smith's CV'. If you are responding to a job posting, the job title and job posting number are necessary, but just a start. Combine this factual information with a little intriguing information, such as:

Financial Analyst no. MB450 – CPA/MBA/8 yrs exp

Posting 2314 – MBA is interested

Job no. 6745 – Top Sales Professional Here

Or if there is no job posting to refer to:

IT Manager – 7 yrs IT Consulting

Fundraiser – Non-profit Exp in Cheltenham

Referral from Tony Banks – Product Management Job

You can also try longer subject lines, for example:

Your next HR Manager – CIPD, FCIPD & Dip PM

A message in your inbox will typically reveal a maximum of 60 characters, the above example is just 56 characters, and an opened message will show up to 150 characters. To be safe, try to get your headline in the first 30 characters,

Your next HR Manager – CIPD, FCIPD

but feel free to use all this extra headline space for a subhead; this example is just 144 characters:

Your next HR Manager – CIPD, FCIPD, Dip PM, HSA. 10 years exp all HR includes arbitration, executive recruitment, selection, compensation, T&D.

All the social networking sites (Facebook, LinkedIn) have special interest groups that are used by recruiters. It is becoming increasingly common for job hunters to post pitches about themselves in the discussion groups. This helps them become visible to recruiters. This is done effectively with just the technique you see above. At 144 characters, this subject line does double duty as an online CV for group discussions.

The same thinking you underwent about extended subject lines applies to your discussion group posts. These aren't the place for 'out-of-the-box-thinking'. Rather, you need hard-hitting statements like this:
    'HR Management – CIPD, FCIPD, Dip PM, HSA, T&D, arbitration, executive recruitment, selection, compensation, restructuring.'

Greeting

It is unprofessional to start an e-mail (or any business communication) without a salutation. There are basic professional courtesies that you must recognize. Don't address the recipient on a first-name basis unless you are already familiar with your contact.

Begin your messages:

Dear Tiffany Carstairs,

Or refer to a specific job, followed by salutation:

Ref Job no. 2376

Dear Ms Carstairs,

Or with any one of the other appropriate greetings we mentioned earlier.

Sign off

End your e-mails with your name followed by contact information:

Thomas Torquemada

12345 678901

Although there is a reply button built into every e-mail program, some people add a hyperlinked (live) e-mail address here on the basis that it encourages a response. If you decide to do so, place it before the telephone number:

Thomas Torquemada
ThomasTorquemada@hotmedia.com
12345 678901

You could also finish with a signature in a script-like font:

Thomas Torquemada
ThomasTorquemada@hotmedia.com
12345 678901

When you receive an e-mail that contains what appears to be a real signature, it makes an impression. However, *you should never use your real signature*; with the littlest bit of technical expertise anyone could copy it, and electronic signatures can have the same legal validity as a written signature. Don't risk your online security for the sake of style. Instead use one of the more legible script fonts. It's a nice touch that most people don't use and becomes part of the branding process that differentiates you. But only do this when everything else about your CV and letter package is complete and consummately professional.

Custom stationery

A number of e-mail programs now support the creation of customized stationery for your e-mails. This is a 'nice to have' look when you are sending directly to an individual and all other aspects of your CV and letter are perfect. There is little point in having fancy e-mail stationery if the wording of your letter is sloppy. It sends entirely the wrong message about who you are as a professional and works against your brand.

If you pursue the option of creating e-mails that look more like traditional business letters, you will follow the same rules for font choice, layout and page colour as you would sending traditional mail communications.

Paste and attach

It is normal when sending CVs without a prior conversation to attach an MSWord/PDF version of your CV and to paste your CV into the e-mail after your signature. You do this because some employers will not open attachments from people they do not know, for fear of viruses. With PDF documents the layout is fixed and will appear exactly as you send it. With MS Word docs the layout sometimes gets messed up. Both ways are acceptable, and there are even people who attach their CV in both formats to give the reader a choice.

Your cover letter will address this by saying, perhaps toward the end of your message,

I have attached my CV in MSWord (or PDF) and also pasted it below the signature for your convenience.

If you are crafting a cover letter for mass distribution, beware of using the mail merge feature of a word-processing program. All too often, the program will fill in the blanks: 'Dear _____' with *italics* (Dear *Fred Jones*) or ***bold italics*** (Dear ***Fred Jones***).

This detracts from all your efforts to be seen in a positive light. All you've achieved is to make it clear that this is a form e-mail, probably sent to thousands of people.

Spell-checking options

You can and should set your e-mails to check spelling before each and every message is sent, but never forget that *automatic spell-check is not completely reliable*.

Before you send any online, or print CV, cover letter or any other job search communication, remember to proofread and get additional outside help in proof-reading. Ask family and friends to review your letter to make sure that what you believe you are sending is received in the way you intended.

Traditional mail still works

Whenever you send your CV by more than one communication medium, it greatly improves your odds. With e-mail as the standard communication medium, most managers get far less traditional mail than they used to, so when you send an e-mail cover letter and also one by traditional mail, you at least *double* your chances of getting your CV read by someone in a position to interview and hire you. We all like to open the mail; it helps us get started at the beginning of the day and fills in those gaps before lunch and as we are winding things down at the end of the work day.

Coordinate your stationery

Letter stationery should always match the colour and weight of your envelopes and CV. Sending a white cover letter – even if it is your personal stationery – with a cream CV detracts from the statement you are trying to make. As for colours, white, cream and grey are all acceptable. Do not use pastel shades unless your target job involves interaction with the very young, aged or infirm where your colour sensitivity may then indicate the personal sensitivity that is relevant with such professions.

Paper quality

The quality of the paper you use matters because it affects the way others perceive you. It tells the recipient something about your values and the importance you attach to the message. This is something that deserves proper attention as an integral part of establishing your professional brand.

All the office supply superstores carry good quality matching CV paper and en-velopes. When you print out CVs, print some letterheads at the same time.

Consistency

Contact information on your letters should be the same as the contact information on your CV and will use the same font. Likewise, the body copy of your letters will use the same font as the body copy on your CV; matching paper and coordinated and complementary fonts indicates a person who proceeds with intent in his or her professional life. It is another subtle way in which you establish a professional brand.

All subsequent letters (follow-up letters after interviews, for example) should be on the same matching paper and envelopes, using the same matching fonts in the same or similar font sizes.

Your written communication is likely to be filed in a candidate dossier. Prior to the hiring decision, a manager will review all the written materials on all the short-list candidates. A thoughtfully packaged written communication aspect of your job search campaign will paint the picture of a thoroughgoing professional, and the sum of your letters will become a powerful and expressive component of the total professional you.

Envelopes send messages, too

What goes on the envelope affects the impact of the message inside. Over the years, I've spoken with countless line managers and human resources professionals about the appearance of the envelopes they receive. Did it affect the likelihood of the letter being read and, if so, with what kind of anticipation? Here's what I heard:

> 'I never open letters with printed pressure-sensitive labels; I regard them as junk mail, and I simply don't have the time in my life for ill-targeted marketing attempts.'

> 'I never open anything addressed to me by title but not by name.'

> 'I will open envelopes and read letters or e-mails addressed to me by misspelled name, but I am looking with a jaundiced eye, keen for other examples of sloppiness.'

> 'I always open correctly typed envelopes that say "personal" and/or "confidential", but if they're not, I feel conned. I don't hire con artists.'

> 'I always open neatly handwritten envelopes. What's more, I open them first, unless there's another letter that is obviously a cheque.'

This last comment is especially interesting in an age when just about all correspondence is printed. In an entirely unscientific test, over a two-week period, every letter I had to send I sent with a hand-addressed envelope, and about 50 per cent of the recipients actually commented on not having seen a handwritten envelope in ages.

If your letter is going by traditional mail and is more than one page, pages should be numbered with contact information on every page.

> I once received an intriguing CV and cover letter. Both had attached to the top right-hand corner a circular red sticker. It worked as a major exclamation point. I was impressed. I was even more impressed when I realized that once this left my hands, no other reader would know exactly who had attached the sticker, but they *would* pay special attention to the contents because of it.

Checklist

Remember that the first glance and feel of your letter can make a powerful impression. The letter's appearance should go hand in hand with its professional-sounding, clear content. Before you seal the envelope, go through this checklist:

Appearance and formatting

❑ Is the paper A4, and is it of good quality with a nice weight to the paper?

❑ Have you used white, off-white, cream or pale grey paper?

❑ Did you use only one side of the page?

❑ Is contact information on every page?

❑ If there is more than one page, have you paginated your letter?

❑ CVs should *not* be stapled to the cover letter.

❑ Did you spell-check and grammar-check and then proofread carefully just to make sure everything's correct?

Content

❏ Does your letter state why you are writing?

❏ Is the letter tied to the target company? Does it refer to a specific job or job posting code when this is relevant?

❏ Is it focused on a target job whenever possible?

❏ Does it include a reference to relevant transferable skills and professional values?

❏ Does it use verbs to show you in action, making a difference with your presence?

❏ Are your most relevant and qualifying experiences prioritized to lend strength to your letter?

❏ Have you avoided wasting more space than needed with employer names and addresses?

❏ Have you omitted any reference to reasons for leaving a particular job? Reasons for making a change might be important at the interview, but they are not relevant at this point. Use this precious space to sell, not to justify.

❏ Unless they have been specifically requested, have you removed all references to past, current or desired salaries?

❏ Have you removed any references to your date of availability?

❏ Do you mention your highest educational attainment only if it is especially relevant and adds credence to the message?

❏ Have you avoided listing irrelevant responsibilities or experience?

❏ Have you given examples of your contributions/achievements, when relevant and possible?

❏ Have you avoided poor focus by eliminating all extraneous information?

❏ Is the letter long enough to whet the reader's appetite for more details, yet short enough not to satisfy that hunger?

❏ Have you let the obvious slip in, like heading your letter 'Letter of Application' in big bold letters? If so, cut it out.

❏ Do you have complete contact information – name, address, postcode, telephone number and e-mail address?

Proofing and printing

It simply isn't possible for even the most accomplished professional writer to go from draft to print, so don't try it. Your pride of authorship will blind you to blemishes you can't afford to miss.

You need some distance from your creative efforts to give yourself detachment and objectivity. There is no hard and fast rule about how long it should take to come up with the finished product. If you think you have finished, leave it alone, at least overnight. Then come back to it fresh. You'll read it almost as if it were meeting your eyes for the first time.

Before you e-mail or print your letters make sure that your writing is as clear as possible. Three things guaranteed to annoy cover letter readers are incorrect spelling, poor grammar and improper syntax. Go back and check all these areas.

The plan of attack

A successful job search needs an integrated overall plan that includes all the most practical job search strategies.

On a call-in radio show during this recession I took a call from a woman who explained that she had sent out almost 300 letters and still wasn't employed. After I asked her a couple of questions, I learned that she had been job-hunting for almost two years and had responded to two or three job postings a week. I also learned that, as an accountant, there were some 2,000 companies for whom she could work.

This job search used only one largely passive approach to finding a job (responding to job postings) when there are at least five practical ways to find work. During her search she managed to approach just 15 per cent of her potential employers in two years. Two employer contacts per week will not get you back to work.

This chapter will focus on tactics that can double, triple and quadruple your chances of getting interviews from job postings by identifying and approaching the people most likely to be in a position to hire you.

Online job postings

When you see a job you can do, respond to the posting in the requested way, but also note all the contact information for the company, including the website and mailing address.

When you can find the names and job titles of managers likely to have a say in the ultimate hiring decision, you can approach them directly in three different ways, each approach increasing your chances of getting an interview:

1 E-mailing your CV directly to that manager with a personalized cover letter doubles your chances of a hit.

2 Sending a CV and personalized cover letter by traditional mail to that manager triples your chances of a hit.

3 Making a follow-up telephone call to that manager first thing in the morning, at lunchtime, or at 5 pm quadruples your chances of a hit.

Internet research tactics for finding names

With a little work you can find the names, titles and contact information for a lot of the people who have the ultimate authority to hire someone like you.

For a start, check out company websites. On the 'about us' pages you can often find names and sometimes contact information for management.

Also try keyword searches on Google, Bing and other search engines. They will all deliver names, and they'll all get different results. Do a standard Google search first, then a Google News search, which looks for mentions of your keywords in media coverage.

When you do a search for a company and find relevant information, you can use it as an opener for your cover letter. Refer to the article and its relevance in your letter. Then copy and paste a URL to the reference if you're sending an e-mail, or enclose a copy of it with a traditional letter.

Try other keyword phrases. You will come up with job openings and job sites. And if you go beyond those first couple of pages of results for your search, which you should always do, drilling down until the well is dry, you will come up with job titles and names to go with those titles.

Why find names?

The more frequently you get into conversation with managers who have the authority to hire you, the faster you will land that new position. In embarking on these conversations, you've skipped over being pulled from the CV database, you have sidestepped the recruiter's evaluation process, and you have the attention of the actual decision maker. You can make a direct and personal pitch.

Your target for a direct approach is always someone who can hire you, although any management position offers an opportunity for referral. For example, while HR people may not have the authority to hire you, the pivotal nature of their work makes them aware of all the areas within a company that could use your skills.

Getting a CV to the 'right someone' by name and making a personalized pitch gives you a distinct advantage; this is never more important than when the economy is weak or in recovery. At such times competition is fierce, and employers always regard initiative and motivation as desirable features.

Who to target in your job search

These are the job titles to target during your job search. As you read, make a list of the specific titles that apply in your professional world, because a list of titles will make it easier to find the names that go with them:

1 Those job titles most likely to be in a position to hire you. Usually one, two and three management positions above you.

2 Other titles likely to have knowledge of an opening:

- management positions one to three levels above you in departments that have an ongoing interaction with your department;

- peers holding similar positions (a little less desirable).

3 Titles most likely to know people involved in the selection process and be able to refer you:

- management positions one to three levels above you in any department;

- internal recruiters and HR professionals.

Any name is better than no name, and with the internet at your fingertips there are endless opportunities to identify the names of people who are in a position to help you.

Networking

One of the best ways to find names and get introductions to employers is to talk to people. And because getting into conversation with the people who can actually offer you a job is the only way you are going to get hired, the more ways you have to get into these conversations, the more successful you are going to be.

When they are integrated into every aspect of your job search, properly executed networking strategies deliver incredible results. We are going to look at some effective ways of building relevant professional networks almost instantly.

Professional associations

One of the best things you can do for your job search and your long-term career success is to become an active member of one or two professional associations. You'll get job leads and a useful network immediately, and such organizations provide great vehicles for increasing your credibility and visibility in the profession. In fact, if you have heard disgruntled job hunters mutter, 'It's not what you know, it's who you know', it probably means they don't understand networking and are probably not members of a professional association.

Associations have monthly meetings in most major areas, plus national get-togethers every year. The local meetings are of immediate interest, and unless you work on a national level, membership in the local branch of a national association will be quite adequate for your needs.

When you join an association and attend the meetings, you get to know and be known by the most committed and best-connected people in your profession. Your membership will help you to stay attuned to what is going on in your profession as associations often offer ongoing training that makes you a more knowledgeable and therefore a more desirable employee.

The professional association is an 'old boy/old girl' network for the modern world. Your membership becomes a link to colleagues, almost all of whom will gladly talk to you, based on your mutual connection through the association.

Most industries and professions have associations, many of which could be valuable, depending on your needs.

If you fit the profile of a special interest or minority group, you will also find professional associations that cater to another dimension of the professional you. These include – but are by no means restricted to – associations for different ethnicities, professionals with disabilities, and women. If you can find a niche association that fits, join that as well: it represents another, even more finely tuned network.

To find appropriate professional associations, try a Google search for relevant keywords. For example, 'legal association' will generate listings of associations for the legal profession; while 'Asian legal association' will generate a listing of local associations for Asian professionals working in the legal field.

When you join an association, you'll benefit greatly from attending the meetings, because this is where you will meet other professionals in your field. But don't just attend the meetings; get involved. Associations are largely volunteer organizations and always need someone to set out chairs or hand out name-tags. The task itself doesn't matter, but your willingness to be an active participant most certainly does and will get you on first-name terms with people you would probably never otherwise meet. Others are more likely to help you when they see you making an effort toward the common good.

It is easier to get to know people than you might think, because all professional association members are there at least in part to advance their careers through networking. You don't have to go straight from introductions to asking for leads on jobs. In fact, it can be more productive to have initial conversations where you make a contribution to the group.

Use the association database or directory

If an association directory comes with your membership package, it will provide you with a superb networking resource for telephone and e-mail networking campaigns.

You can feel comfortable calling any other member on the phone and introducing yourself: 'Hi, Brenda Massie? My name is Martin Yate. We haven't spoken before, but we are both members of the Teachers Association. I need some advice; can you spare a minute?'

Your mutual membership will guarantee you a few moments of anyone's time, a courtesy you should always return.

You can also use the directory to generate introductions for jobs you have heard about elsewhere. For example, you might have found an interesting job posting on www.careerbuilder.co.uk, or perhaps on a company website, with the request that you upload your CV. Apply as requested, then turn to your membership directory to find people who work for that company.

A judicious call or two will frequently get you a personal referral and some inside information, and you have doubled your chances of landing that interview. Once you have an interview, these same contacts can help you prepare for it with insider knowledge about the company, the department and the manager.

Professional associations all have online newsletters and many have a jobs section on their website, where companies advertise because of the suitably quali-fied response. So you will often see job postings there that don't appear anywhere else. In difficult economic times, a savvy employer will use an association website to skim the cream of available talent while screening out the less committed. You will also notice that association members write the articles in the newsletters. As everyone likes to have their literary efforts appreciated, telling a member you have read an article that he or she has written gives you a great introduction to a network-ing call or letter.

Active association membership puts you on the radar of all the best-qualified and connected professionals in your area. You can also list it at the end of your CV under a Professional Affiliations heading. This is guaranteed to get a second glance, as it signifies professional awareness. Employers and headhunters will sometimes use words like association, club and society in their keyword searches, so associa-tion membership will also help to get your CV pulled up from the databases for investigation by human eyes.

How to make networking work

Professional associations are just one of a dozen approaches for networking, all of which can be tremendously beneficial to your job search and overall career success, if you nurture them.

Think of networking as professional connectedness, because becoming properly connected to your profession is the activity that will generate the widest range of relevant contacts for your job search.

An effective job search requires more than writing to and chatting with old cronies on the telephone. It's important to move beyond your personal network of friends and acquaintances because you may well discover that your network is not as comprehensive as you might have wished.

Besides, just because you worked with someone five years ago doesn't mean he or she still regards you as a friend, especially if you haven't spoken to that person since then. Surveys show that we all respond in these understandable ways:

- To those requests from people I didn't know, I asked for a CV (of course, if they had an introduction or were fellow members of an association, things would be different).

- If I received it in good time with a thoughtfully prepared accompanying letter, I would give that person help if I could.

- To requests from people with an introduction from someone I liked and respected, I gave time and consideration and, wherever possible, assistance.

- To requests from friends, people I had worked with at one time and who had kept in touch since we had worked together, I provided leads and even made calls on their behalf.

- To requests from people who regarded themselves as friends but who had not maintained contact, or who had only re-established contact when they wanted something: for some reason I was unable to help them. I wished them the best of luck, but, 'Sorry I couldn't help you. If something comes to mind, I'll be sure to call.'

Nothing works like a personal recommendation from a fellow professional – and you get that by being a fellow professional, by being connected to your profession, the professionals within it and by becoming a colleague – someone who shares. It is no accident that successful people in all fields know each other; they helped each other become successful because they stayed in touch, through good times and bad, and helped each other whenever they could.

If you are going to use business colleagues and personal friends in your job search, don't do it half-heartedly. We live in a mobile society, so in addition to family, friends and the colleagues you know naturally, it is a smart long-term career management strategy to establish yourself as a member of your professional community.

Social networking

Social networking has become an integral part of cutting-edge job search and career management strategies. It revolves around social and/or professionally oriented online networks that help you reach out to people you know, once knew, or would like to know. You can extend your professional reach by connecting with others in your field, along with people with whom you share common experiences or interests.

You will find social networking sites especially important when you are planning a career change. If you know you are moving out of one profession and into another, you can use social networking sites to build a network of people who do the target job in your chosen profession and, whenever possible, people who have made a similar transition.

Here's an example: a soldier who was leaving the army sought my help in her search for a new civilian career. First, to find other individuals with a similar background, I put in the word army at www.linkedin.com, the online networking site. I got more than 4,000 profiles of people who shared her military experience. We then tried a search using the phrase 'information technology' (her desired career change) and got 39,000 profiles. Both these potential networks would have relevance to her job search, but it got even better when we combined both the keywords: 'information technology and army'. This pulled up 908 profiles of people who shared her life experience and who had, in about half the hits, already made the transition to her desired profession. Such a degree of initial connectivity ensured she could hold helpful conversations with an enormous number of people, each of whom could be relevant to her job search.

Social networking sites are seen by recruiters and headhunters, and this should shape the information you make available about yourself.

For the professional in a job search this will start with simply cutting and pasting your CV into your official profile. You make yourself visible but because this is a social networking site and not a CV bank you do it without an 'I'm for sale' sign, which is useful when you are employed and looking for a new position.

Social networking can get you useful introductions to people throughout your profession, the country and the world – people who might know of jobs at their own companies or who can introduce you to people at companies that have openings. This new application of technology enables you to reach out into an almost limitless community of like-minded professionals.

It works simply: you join a social networking site and find people you have worked with in the past. Then expand your network by joining the discussion groups that exist on all social networking sites and then connect with other members of those groups.

For employers and recruiters, networking sites constitute a reliable pathway to recruit qualified candidates, while for a job hunter they constitute a reliable pathway to jobs through the people connected to them. You can search a site's database by location, job title, company or any keywords of your choice. The database will pull up the profiles of people who match your requirements and allow you to initiate contact directly, through your common membership in groups or through the chain of people who connect you.

There are just too many sites to list, and the more they proliferate, the more specialized they become. It is probably a good idea to have a presence on two of the biggest, linkedin.com and facebook.com, but you'll also find networking sites for special interests, languages, gender, race and more.

A very smart networking idea

Intelligent networking encourages you to form relationships with people in your profession and industry at many levels. Almost anyone in your industry or location can be useful regardless of position or experience, but the people of most interest will probably fall into these categories:

1 Those who are one to three levels above you, who might hire you, now or in the future. With this group you can initiate contact by sending an e-mail to introduce yourself and ask him/her to look at your profile. If this proceeds to a conversation and interviews, fine; if not, you can ask your contact to connect you to others.

2 Those at or below your level but with similar professional experience.

3 Those who work in related areas within the same profession or industry.

It's best to build a relationship by finding common ground. You can initiate relationships by asking for advice, and many people will give you a few minutes of their time. You will develop the best relationships, though, by reaching out to others with help and advice, because when you offer something, forging a relationship with you becomes important to the other person. It is easy to do this by taking an active part in the special interest groups and also searching the social sites for people in your profession who are actively looking for jobs.

The challenge then becomes how to encourage a relationship that shares introductions and job leads. The answer is logical and painless: use the job leads you hear about that are inappropriate for your own use.

It's a not-so-funny thing about the job search: when you are just out of school no one is hiring entry-level workers; they all want you to call back in five years.

Five years later when you are once again looking for a job, they now only want someone just out of school or with 10 years' experience.

In your job search activities you are constantly coming across positions that aren't right for you but that could be just what someone else is aching to hear about. Offer these leads to others as part of your introduction. Here's how it can work: sometimes you have to send an e-mail stating why you want to make contact, and sometimes you can communicate immediately – it depends on a number of variables. In the first instance you send an e-mail simply stating you have a job lead that he or she might find interesting. This is a nice gesture and will get you lots of introductions.

In the second instance, where you are actually in direct e-mail communication, state your business: 'I am involved in a strategic career move right now, and I have come across a job that isn't right for me but which could be perfect for you. If you'd like to talk, let's exchange telephone numbers. I'll be happy to pass the lead on, and perhaps you have heard about something that would suit me... I am moving into the private sector and have been looking for jobs in IT in the South... .'

(When networking, never talk about what you want in that ideal next job. It reduces the odds of someone telling you about an opening. Instead, talk about what you can do.)

Your job search has you scouring the job sites for job leads, and now you have a use for all those positions that aren't quite right for you. Build your own database of the jobs that are not suitable for you and pass them on to all those people above and below you in your profession who will make symbiotic networking partners.

How social networks expand your options

When you find suitable jobs on the job sites, you are usually faced with uploading your CV into a company or headhunter's database, but now, along with your professional association memberships, your social networks give you additional approaches. Somewhere on one of your social networking sites there are people who work at that company, either now or in the past. Search for them, using the company name in your keyword search, then look for job titles one, two and three levels above your own, and then those at the same level or one or two beneath you.

The more you reach out, the better your reputation becomes and the more others will reach out to you.

Networking letters

When you write networking e-mails and letters, use these guidelines for your structure. You can also use them as frameworks for networking conversations:

1 Establish a connection, something or someone in common or information likely to be of interest.

2 You can use your common membership in professional associations as a bridge to other members.

3 Let contacts know what you can do. They will invariably want to help, but you have to give them a framework to target their effort. DO NOT tell them about your dream job, or the promotion you hope for; talking about dreams only reduces their options to help.

4 Try to be specifically vague: 'I'm looking for something in operations within the medical devices area' gives the listener the widest possible opportunity for coming up with leads.

5 Tell whoever you are writing or calling: 'It's time for me to make a move' or 'My job just got sent to Mumbai, and I'm hoping I could pick your brain.'

6 Don't ask specifically, 'Can you hire me?' or 'Can your company hire me?' Ask for advice and leads. Then ask for guidance.

7 By all means ask for leads within specific target companies, but don't rely on a contact with a particular company to get you in.

8 When you do get help, say thank you. And if you get the help verbally, follow it up in writing. The impression is indelible, and it just might get you another lead.

When you write networking letters and make the follow-up calls, you might be surprised to find out who your friends are: someone you always regarded as a real mate won't give you the time of day, and someone you never thought of as a friend will go above and beyond the call of duty on your behalf.

Names increase your options

Sometimes, to alert all the right people at a target company that you're available you might approach half a dozen different managers. For example, let's say you are a young engineer enthusiastic about a job with Last Chance Electronics. It is within the bounds of reason that you would submit a cover letter and CV to any or all of the following people, with each letter addressed by name to minimize its chances of going straight into the bin:

- Managing Director;

- Director of engineering;

- Chief engineer;

- Engineering design manager;

- Head of Human Resources;

- Technical engineering manager.

Think through all the titles likely to be of use to you, based on the above criteria, and keep all these titles in mind when you go looking for names to attach to them: the more options you have, the more results you will get.

Sending out your cover letters

E-mail and traditional mail initiatives should be integrated into every aspect of your job search. They should be a vital part of your job search strategy. Maintain a balance between the number of e-mails and letters you send out on a daily and weekly basis and the types of letters you send out. Follow them up by making telephone calls to initiate the conversations that must take place if you are to get job offers.

Do you need to compose more than one letter?

Almost certainly, there is a case for having letters targeted at all your specific needs: to headhunters, to managers referencing job postings, to managers without reference to a specific job, letters referencing a referral, and networking letters, to name but a few. The key is to do a great master version of each that you can customize as needed.

A plan for a direct approach

A professionally conducted campaign will target the employers most likely to hire you and use e-mail and traditional mail for the initial approach, followed by a phone call.

Scary I know, but it works, and I'll give you advice for doing it shortly.

As you identify target companies, create a folder for each one; the next time you need to make a strategic career move, having details of the area's desirable employers is one of the many ways you will be ahead of the game.

As you discover names to go with job titles, send a personalized cover letter and CV via e-mail and traditional mail and schedule a follow-up telephone call in your week's agenda.

Send further CVs and personalized cover letters as you find other people within that company. You might also consider bookmarking desirable companies to check their job openings.

This is not your last job search

This is probably not the first or the last job search you will ever do, so save all your job search letters in a career management folder where you can find them again when you need them.

Develop electronic documents or paper file folders containing all the relevant information for each company. You'll want a link to the website and a list of the names of the company's executives and all other management names and titles that you have identified as relevant to your job search. Whenever you find interesting information, copy it into the company folder. For instance, you might come across information on growth or shrinkage in a particular area of a company, or you might read about recent acquisitions the company has made. You can use websites such as Google and Google News to track company activities.

All this information will help you target potential employers. Your knowledge will create a favourable impression when you first contact the company: that you made an effort is noticed and sets you apart from other applicants who don't bother. It says that you respect the company, the opportunity and the interviewer; these perceptions help you to stand out.

All your efforts have an obvious short-term value in helping you generate job interviews and offers. Who would you interview and subsequently hire? The person who knows nothing about your company, or the person who knows everything and shows enthusiasm with that knowledge?

Your efforts also have long-term value, because you are building a personalized reference work of your industry/speciality/profession so you can hit the ground running the next time you wish to make a job change.

Follow-up: a cautionary tale

If you sit there like Buddha waiting for the world to beat a path to your door, you may wait a long time.

A friend of mine placed an advertisement for an analyst. Within a week he had received more than 100 responses. Ten days later he'd received 50 more and was still ploughing through them when he received a follow-up call (the only one he did receive) from one of the candidates who'd tracked down his name. The candidate's CV was languishing in the pile with all the others, but the follow-up phone call got it discovered.

The job hunter was in the office by the end of the day. She returned the following morning, and was hired by lunchtime. This is not an isolated incident. It happens all the time. Candidates who make themselves visible get hired.

Managers are always on the lookout for competent professionals in their field, BUT they hate recruiting and interviewing. They just want to find the right person, hire him or her, and get back to work. All you have to do is help them by using the tactics outlined in this book.

Follow-up calls work

You'll notice that some examples in the letter section mention that the applicant will follow up with a phone call. This allows the writer to explain to any inquisitive receptionist that Joe Smith is 'expecting my call' or that it is 'personal', or 'it's accounting/engineering/customer-service business'.

It's surprising that so many people are nervous about calling a fellow professional on the phone and talking about what they do for a living. Don't worry so much. In this unsettled world, there is an unwritten credo shared by the vast majority of professional people: you should always help one another if it isn't going to hurt you in the process. Everyone out there has been in your situation and knows it can happen at any moment. Because of this, almost everyone you speak to will be sympathetic to your cause and help you if they can.

No manager will take offence at a call from a professional colleague, and this is what you are.

Use a contact tracker

To ensure that you keep track of your mailings and the follow-up phone calls, I recommend that you create a Contact Tracker on a spreadsheet program such as Microsoft Excel. Create columns for the company name, telephone number, e-mail address and contact name. As a rule of thumb, an e-mail sent today is ripe for follow-up within 24 to 48 hours; a letter posted today is ripe for follow-up three to five days later.

Cover letters: the key to your job search

Nine out of ten managers prefer a cover letter with a CV, so a great cover letter will get your CV read with serious attention. It will set you apart and increase the number of interviews you get. You'll even have more productive and successful interviews because the interviewer will have a better idea of who you are professionally and who you are as a person.

The sample letter section that follows includes many types of job search letters that you can use throughout your job search. Use them to help you stand out at every step of the selection process.

Sample letters

Here's the real meat and potatoes of the book – the sample letters you can use as models for your own.

E-mail response to online job posting (technical sales representative)

From: Joan Carter [jcartersalespro@hotmail.com]
To: Recipient's e-mail address
Cc:
Subject: Tech sales/key acct/new territory dev/negotiation/customer service

Dear Recipient's Name,

I wish to apply for the Technical Sales Representative position currently available with your company, as listed on Monster.co.uk. My confidential CV is attached for your review and consideration, and I believe you will find me well qualified.

In my CV you will find a solid background in Sales and Marketing, with over two years in technical sales. In this capacity, I have developed an expertise in new and key account acquisition, new territory development and management, contract negotiation and customer service. I am confident that my experience in these areas will prove to be an asset to ABC Ltd.

I am familiar with blueprints, part number breakdowns and the bidding process of our major accounts, which include _____, _____, _____ and _____. I have doubled my sales from £40,000/month to £80,000/month in just two years, and I am known for effectively identifying and resolving problems before they affect related areas, personnel or customers.

I welcome the opportunity to discuss with you how I might make similar contributions to the success of ABC Ltd. I look forward to hearing from you to arrange a personal interview.

Yours sincerely,

Joan Carter
12345 678901
Attachment: CV

E-mail response to online job posting (investment banker)

From: James Stratton [jsinvest@anyserver.co.uk]
To: Recipient's e-mail address
Cc:
Subject: Administrative Investment Banker job posting

Dear Recipient's Name,

I am responding to the Administrative Investment Banker job posting on your company's website. I have attached my CV for your consideration.

My experience as an administrative investment banker and assistant to a Director is, I believe, readily adaptable to your needs. I have spent five years in a position best described as 'doing whatever needs to be done' and have capitalized on my ability to undertake a large and widely varied array of projects, learn quickly, find effective solutions to problems, and maintain a sense of humour throughout.

My years as an administrative professional have also provided me with an unusual sensitivity to the needs of senior professionals. I have substantial computer experience and am fully computer literate. I have been told my verbal and written communication skills are exceptional.

I believe your firm would provide a working atmosphere to which I would be well suited, as well as one where my diverse experience would be valuable.

My salary requirements are reasonable and negotiable based on the responsibilities and opportunities presented.

Yours sincerely,

James Stratton
12345 678901
Attachment: CV

E-mail response to online job posting
(legal administrator)

From: Helen Darvik [darviklegalpro@earthlink.net]
To: Recipient's e-mail address
Cc:
Subject: Administrator/mgmnt/mktg/cmptr/acctg/planning/personnel

Dear Recipient's Name,

I am responding to your job posting on Hotjobs.co.uk for a legal administrator of a law firm. I wrote to you on (date) about law administrator positions in the _____ area. I have attached another CV of my educational background and employment history. I am very interested in this position.

I have been a legal administrator for two law firms during the past six years. In addition, I have been a law firm consultant for over a year. Besides my law firm experience, I have been a medical administrator for over 10 years. I believe that all of this experience will enable me to manage this position very successfully. I possess the management, marketing, computer, accounting/budgeting, financial planning, personnel and people-oriented skills that will have a very positive impact on this law firm.

I will be in the _____ area later in the month and hope we can meet at that time to discuss this position. I look forward to hearing from you, Ms _____, concerning this position. Thank you for your time and consideration.

Yours sincerely,

Helen Darvik
12345 678901
Attachment: CV

E-mail response to online job posting (manufacturing)

Murray shows loyalty, depth of experience in several positions, reliability and accomplishments, as well as his well-earned reputation.

From: Murray Danton [manufacturerMD@mindspring.com]
To: Recipient's e-mail address
Cc:
Subject: Warehouse pro: 26 years' inventory control, import/export, shipping, tracking, organization

Dear Recipient's Name,

You are seeking an experienced and self-motivated warehouse manager. For the past 26 years, I have been working successfully in manufacturing and warehouse settings. I am a hard-working employee who always looks for ways to improve productivity, efficiency and accuracy. A warehouse manager for 12 years, in my current position I have identified ways to reduce downtime and waste, as well as methods to increase production using my extensive background in material handling, shipping, receiving and warehousing. Throughout my career, I have demonstrated my loyalty, commitment to excellence and solid work ethic. I am confident that I will make an immediate and long-term contribution to your company.

Throughout my career I have been dedicated to the principles of quality, continuous improvement and customer satisfaction. My supervisor has noted my record of 'excellent attendance and dependability' and praised me as 'reliable and highly motivated'.

I would like to meet you to discuss my qualifications. Please call me at the following phone number, or leave a message, to arrange an interview. Thank you for your consideration.

Yours faithfully,

Murray Danton
12345 678901
Attachment: CV

E-mail response to online job posting (production supervisor)

From: Edwin Pastore [productionpro@yahoo.com]
To: Recipient's e-mail address
Cc:
Subject: Production Super matches your exact requirements

Dear Recipient's Name,

I am writing in response to the job posting on your company's website. Please consider my CV in your search for a Production Supervisor.

With a hi-tech background in FTSE 100 companies, I feel well qualified for the position you described. I am presently responsible for the coordination of production in three assembly and test areas that employ 35 personnel. Maintaining control of work of this magnitude and complexity requires my ability to function independently, and a willingness to make decisions quickly and effectively.

I am accustomed to a fast-paced environment where deadlines are a priority and handling multiple jobs simultaneously is the norm. I enjoy a challenge and work hard to attain my goals. Constant negotiations with all levels of management and employees have strengthened my interpersonal skills. I would very much like to discuss with you how I could contribute to your organization.

I am seeking an opportunity to excel in a more dynamic company and am looking forward to relocating to the _____ area.

Please contact me at your earliest convenience so that I can clarify my background and enthusiasm for the job. Thank you for your time and consideration.

Yours sincerely,

Edwin Pastore
12345 678901
Attachment: CV

E-mail response to newspaper advertisement (health care management)

This applicant wants to change to an administrative position in the field of health care; thus we highlighted her leadership and administrative skills.

From: Reba Woodward [rwoodward@email.com]
To: Recipient's e-mail address
Cc:
Subject: Administrative Health Care Services

Dear Recipient's Name,

I am a registered nurse with a background as programme director, school nurse, operating room circulator, and charge nurse in clinic, A&E and hospital floor environments. The following skills and characteristics are reason to take a closer look at my credentials. I am:

- **strong in handling multiple tasks and multifaceted situations while maintaining satisfactory interpersonal relationships with staff, physicians, patients, students and families;**

- **an expert at ensuring compliance with regulations while keeping costs within budget;**

- **talented in prioritizing issues and tasks and visualizing the 'big' picture when considering the long-term effects of my decisions;**

- **an outcome-orientated self-starter with superior organizational and administrative skills.**

After reviewing my CV, you will discover that my qualifications are a good match for this position. The opportunity for a personal interview to discuss employment possibilities further would be mutually beneficial. You can reach me on 12345 678901 to arrange an appointment. In the meantime, thank you for your time and consideration.

Yours sincerely,

Reba Woodward
012345 67890
Attachment: CV

Response to newspaper advertisement (speech therapy position)

A speech therapist is looking for a position in a community college.

Harriette L Christophorous

12345 678901   1 Any Street   harrichris@anyserver.co.uk
Anytown AA1 1AA

12 January 20–

Ms Alexandra Kinkead
Director of Human Resources
Anytown Community College
1000 Any Avenue
Anytown AA1 1AA

Dear Ms Kinkead,

Your recent advertisement has captured my serious interest. I am confident that my 25 years' experience as a Speech Therapist at the ABC Centre provides me with the capabilities to fulfil the **Voice & Articulation** position mentioned in the ad. Accordingly, I have enclosed a CV that briefly outlines my professional history.

Some key points you may find relevant to this opportunity include:

✓ *Experience assessing needs of and providing instruction to the disabled. In my current position, I work one-on-one with students having hearing loss, emotional disorders, ADHD, autism, and other physical disabilities impacting their ability to acquire speech. I also develop IEPs and participate in the CSE process to define students' needs and implement instruction plans.*

✓ *Excellent leadership skills, with experience mentoring co-workers. Currently, I mentor speech therapists and teachers working with hearing-impaired students, as well as direct the activities of two other speech therapists.*

✓ *A master's degree in Speech Pathology, plus Certification as a Speech & Hearing Handicapped Teacher. In addition, I have attended workshops in Phonemic Awareness, Autism, and Pervasive Developmental Disorders.*

In my current role, I am accountable for addressing the needs of approximately 300 elementary and secondary school students with various speech deficiencies. I believe that my knowledge and expertise would allow me to serve your students effectively in this Voice & Articulation instructional role. I would enjoy speaking to you in person to discuss in more detail how my qualifications can fulfil your needs. Please contact me via phone or e-mail to arrange a mutually convenient date and time for us to meet.

Thank you for your time and consideration. I look forward to talking to you soon.

Yours sincerely,

Harriette L Christophorous

Harriette L Christophorous

Enclosure: CV

E-mail response to newspaper advertisement (hydrogeologist)

Applying for positions in a newly emerging scientific discipline, this candidate's CV requires a heavy emphasis on educational background information.

From: Aileen Renfro [arenfro@email.com]
To: Recipient's e-mail address
Cc:
Subject: Hydrogeologist/Groundwater Modeller: Solute transport modelling, quantitative skills

RE: Position of Hydrogeologist/Groundwater Modeller, Company Job ID: ACHZ4121-234059, AJB Reference Number: 4950495, Job ID #0000BZ/BBBB

Dear Recipient's Name,

I learned about your position for a Hydrogeologist/Groundwater Modeller with great interest, as my qualifications match your requirements for this position almost exactly. Please accept my CV for your review and allow me to explain briefly how I can contribute to ABC Ltd.

With an MSc in Hydrologic Sciences and over 7 years' research experience, I have developed a strong background in advanced theories of solute transport modelling. Consequently, I have developed effective quantitative skills and a practical understanding of the fundamental principles and concepts associated with hydrogeology.

My CV will provide additional details regarding my educational background and professional experience. Beyond these qualifications, it may be helpful for you to know that I have worked successfully in both independent and team project environments, adapt readily to rapidly changing work conditions, and enjoy the prospect of contributing to ABC's '80-year reputation as a water industry leader' in the advancement of hydrogeologic and groundwater projects.

I would welcome the opportunity to be interviewed for this position and to discuss the results you can expect from me as a member of your team. Thank you for your time and consideration.

Yours sincerely,

Aileen Renfro
0123456 7890
Attachment: CV

Response to newspaper advertisement (customer service representative)

An ad response with requested salary history.

Cassidy Stratton
1 Any Street • Anytown AA1 1AA • 12345 678901 • cassidy123@custsrv.net

---

4 February 20–

Mr Josh Williams
Personnel Director
ABC Financial Group
111 Any Avenue
Anytown AA1 1AA

Dear Mr Williams,

In response to your advertisement in *Newsday* for a customer service representative, I am forwarding my CV for your review and consideration. Ideally, this position will make optimal use of my experience working in capacities that require strong interpersonal communication and customer needs assessment skills, an ability to interface effectively with internal/external contacts, and a skill for ensuring the accurate, timely processing of electronic, verbal and written information.

Since 1994, I have held longstanding positions of increased responsibility for leading financial services organizations, in charge of tracking, monitoring, reviewing and processing account and market-related data. In these positions, I have proved and continue to prove myself a capable, take-charge team player with an ability to coordinate diversified departmental and customer support functions. Combined with my ability to manage and train others proficiently on the complexities of comprehensive databases and improve workflow efficiencies, I am confident that I would be an asset to your customer service organization.

I would welcome the opportunity to meet you for an in-depth interview. Thank you for your review and consideration. I look forward to hearing from you soon.

Yours sincerely,

Cassidy Stratton

Cassidy Stratton

Salary Requirement:
£36,000 – £44,000

Salary History:
XYZ Financial Group: Starting £29,000; Ending £40,000
Credit Checkers: Starting £20,000; Ending £26,000
Enclosure: CV

E-mail response to newspaper advertisement (sales associate)

An entry-level cover letter to convince the employer that he can tackle a full-time job even though he is still in college.

From: Mark Lombardi [mlombardi@email.com]
To: Recipient's e-mail address
Cc:
Subject: Sales Associate with verifiable track record

Dear Recipient's Name,

If you are searching for a success-driven Sales Associate with a verifiable track record, look no further. Highlights of my achievements include:

- Awarded end-of-year bonus and commended for exemplary sales performance.

- Started a business from scratch and increased customer base using multiple marketing methods.

- Earned most of my own college expenses for the last four years.

Although I will not graduate until December, I am eager to start work as soon as possible – either full- or part-time. I can balance the responsibilities of a Sales Associate position with my studies, because I have successfully done so with a full course load in the past.

My CV is attached for your consideration. I believe that I can make a positive contribution to ABC Sports Outfitters and look forward to discussing my qualifications in detail.

I will call you next week to arrange for a meeting at a mutually convenient time. Thank you for your consideration.

Yours sincerely,

Marc Lombardi
0123456 7890
Attachment: CV

Response to newspaper advertisement (skilled labourer)

This cover letter had to overcome an obvious 'overqualification' barrier.

JACK Levan

1 Any Street • Anytown AA1 1AA • jlevan555@yahoo.com • 12345 878901

Tuesday, 11 November 20–

Mr Drake Norris
ABC Ltd
111 Any Avenue
Anytown AA1 1AA

Dear Mr Norris,

When I saw your announcement for a skilled labourer at ABC Ltd, I made writing this letter my first priority. Of course, I've already applied online. But, the more I thought about this opportunity, the more it seemed a perfect match for both of us. And so I wanted you to have a good deal more than the usual, impersonal, application.

I think you deserve to see the contributions I can make to the ABC team at once. That's why you'll find my CV different from others you may have come across. In place of the usual 'objective statement', you'll read about four productivity-building capabilities I can bring to the job. And, right below them, are seven examples of the kinds of contributions I've made to my employers.

But I am concerned that you may think I am 'overqualified'. To put that in plain language, you may feel I will be bored by the job. In fact, your position fits well with my goal of getting my degree in Aerospace Engineering. I can't think of a better opportunity to see the OT&E process at work than being 'in the trenches' on a project like yours.

I do best when I can learn about my employer's special needs. May I call in a few days to explore how I might fit your team?

Yours sincerely,

Jack Levan

Jack Levan

Enclosure: CV

Response to newspaper advertisement (assessment coordinator)

Anna M Sanchez

111 Any Street • Anytown AA1 1AA • 12345 678901 • Mobile 1098765 4321

2 PAGES VIA FAX   11 June 20–
DEPT. HD 212-555-9999

Your advertisement in the *Times*, on 9 June 20–, for an **Assessment Coordinator** seems to match my background and experience perfectly. As the International Brand Coordinator for ABC, I coordinated meetings, prepared presentations and materials, organized a major off-site conference, and supervised an assistant. I believe that I am an excellent candidate for this position as I have illustrated below:

YOUR REQUIREMENTS	MY QUALIFICATIONS
A highly motivated, diplomatic, flexible, quality-driven professional on every project.	Successfully managed project teams involving different business units. The defined end results were achieved.
Exceptional organizational skills and attention to detail.	Planned the development and launch of the ABC Heritage Edition series. My former manager enjoyed leaving the 'details' and follow-through to me. Project management training.
Degree and minimum 3 years' relevant business experience.	BA from City University. 5+ years' business experience in productive, professional environments.
Computer literacy.	Extensive knowledge of Windows & Macintosh applications.

I'm interested in this position because it fits well with my new career focus in the human resources field. Currently, I am enrolled in City College's Adult Career Planning and Development certificate programme and working at XYZ Ltd.

I have enclosed my CV to provide more information on my strengths and career achievements. If after reviewing my material you believe that there is a match, please call me. Thank you for your consideration.

Yours sincerely,

Anna M Sanchez

Anna M Sanchez

Enclosure: CV

E-mail response to newspaper advertisement (office administrator)

From: Mark Stevenson [mstevenson@email.com]
To: Recipient's e-mail address
Cc:
Subject: Office Administrator job posting

Dear Recipient's Name,

Your advertisement for an **Office Administrator** caught my attention because my background appears to parallel your needs.

I am **self-sufficient** and **able to work independently with little supervision**. I am regarded as **an information resource** and enjoy sharing my knowledge with others. I also have extensive experience **managing projects** and **planning meetings, trips and special events**.

Process streamlining is a strength. I have **developed software-based systems and processes** to automate production reporting, notify customers of changes and inform the field staff of company directives. When supervising clerical staff, I always try to **plan ahead** to make the best use of their time.

I work well with executives, sales representatives, customers, vendors *and* co-workers, and demonstrate strong interpersonal communication skills and good judgement. I always try to listen closely and understand what others need. Then, I look for ways to help solve the problem.

I am confident that I can deliver results for ABC Ltd. My CV is attached for your review. Thank you for your time and consideration; I look forward to speaking with you soon.

Yours sincerely

Mark Stevenson
0123456 7890
Attachment: CV

E-mail response to newspaper advertisement (legal secretary)

From: Marianne Johnston [mjohnston@email.com]
To: Recipient's e-mail address
Cc:
Subject: Bar Council Legal Secretary

RE: GENERAL COUNCIL OF THE BAR, LEGAL SECRETARY

Dear Recipient's Name,

It is with continued interest and enthusiasm that I respond to your advertisement for Legal Secretary to the General Council of the Bar. I believe that my education and experience combine to create a perfect match for the position, and would appreciate careful consideration of my credentials as presented below and within my CV, attached.

Although a relative newcomer to the field, I have earned my HNC in Legal Studies and Paralegal certificate. With more than two years' experience after qualifying, providing administrative and clerical support in private practice, I am confident that I possess the expertise and dedication that will make an immediate and significant contribution to the efficiency and organization of the Council.

It has long been my dream to pursue a career in the legal arena, and my goal to associate with the top professionals in the field. Where better to continue my professional development than within the heart of the organization as a provider of administrative support to members of the Bar itself.

If you are looking for a legal support professional who is committed to the highest standards of performance, relates well with others, is self-directing and highly motivated, and is looking for a long-term employment relationship, please contact me to arrange an interview. I will make myself available at your earliest convenience.

Thank you for your consideration; I look forward to the opportunity to speak to you soon.

Yours sincerely,

Marianne Johnston
012345 67890
Attachment: CV and Professional References

Response to newspaper advertisement (accounting manager)

Paul Anthony

12345 678901   1 Any Street   accountingpro@anyserver.co.uk
                                               Anytown AA1 1AA

(Date)

Phillip _____
(Title)
ABC Ltd
1 Industry Plaza
Anytown AA1 1AA

Dear Mr _____,

Re: File No. 213

I have six years' accounting experience and am responding to your recent advertisement for an Accounting Manager. Please allow me to highlight my skills as they relate to your stated requirements.

Your Requirements	My Experience
• A recognized accounting qualification plus several years of practical experience	• Obtained CIMA membership and have over three years' experience as an Accounting Manager.
• Excellent people skills and demonstrated ability to motivate staff	• Effectively managed a staff of 24 including two supervisors.
• Strong administrative and analytical skills	• Assisted in the development of a base reference library with Microsoft Excel for 400 clients.
• Good oral and written communication skills	• Trained four new supervisors via daily coaching sessions, communication meetings and technical skill sessions.

I believe this background provides the management skills you require. This position sounds interesting and I would welcome the opportunity for a personal interview to discuss my qualifications further.

Yours sincerely,

Paul Anthony

Paul Anthony

Enclosure: CV

Response to newspaper advertisement (international sales manager)

Suzanne A Kennedy
1 Any Street
Anytown AA1 1AA
12345 678901

(Date)

Phillip _____
(Title)
ABC Ltd
1 Industry Plaza
Anytown AA1 1AA

Dear Mr _____,

Re: International Sales Manager, *Globe & Mail*, – September 20–

I was recently speaking to Mr _____ from your company and he strongly recommended that I send you a copy of my CV. Knowing the requirements for the position, he felt that I would be an ideal candidate. For more than 11 years, I have been involved in international sales management, with seven years directly in the aerospace industry. My qualifications for the position include:

- establishing sales offices in France, Great Britain and Germany;
- recruiting and managing a group of 24 international sales representatives;
- providing training programmes for all of the European staff, which included full briefings on our own products as well as competitor lines;
- obtaining 42 per cent, 33 per cent and 31 per cent of the French, German and British markets, respectively, dealing with all local engine and airframe manufacturers; and
- generating more than £32 million in sales with excellent margins.

My Bachelor of Science degree in electrical engineering was obtained at the University of _____ and my languages include French and German.

I feel confident that an interview would demonstrate that my expertise in setting up rep organizations and training and managing an international sales department would be an excellent addition to your growing aerospace corporation.

I look forward to meeting you, Mr _____, and will give you a call to follow up on this letter the week of (date) _____.

Yours sincerely,

Suzanne A Kennedy

Suzanne A Kennedy

Enclosure: CV

Response to newspaper advertisement (executive assistant)

Andrew F Petersen

1 Any Street • Anytown AA1 1AA

12345 678901 • executiveassistant@localnet.com

(Date)

Box 9412
Anytown AA1 1AA

Dear Recipient's Name,

I was very pleased to learn of the need for an Executive Assistant in your company from your recent advertisement in _____. I believe the qualities you seek are well matched by my track record:

Your Needs	My Qualifications
Independent Self-Starter	• Served as company liaison between sales representatives, controlling commissions and products.
	• Controlled cash flow, budget planning and bank reconciliation for three companies.
	• Assisted in the promotion of a restaurant within a private placement sales effort, creating sales materials and communicating with investors.
Computer Experience	• Used Lotus in preparing financial spreadsheet used in private placement memoranda and Macintosh to design brochures and flyers.
	• Have vast experience with both computer programming and the current software packages.
Compatible Background	• Spent five years overseas and speak French.
	• Served as an executive assistant to four corporate heads.

A CV is enclosed that covers my experience and qualifications in greater detail. I would appreciate the opportunity to discuss my credentials in a personal interview.

Yours sincerely,

Andrew Petersen

Andrew Petersen

Enclosure: CV

E-mail response to online job posting (teaching position)

This instructor was awarded the position she aspired to.

From: Sarah Anne Steel [sasteel@email-com]
To: Recipient's e-mail address
Cc:
Subject: Jewellery Repair and Design Tutor

Dear Recipient's Name,

I am very interested in your recently posted **Jewellery Repair and Design Tutor position**.
I was thrilled to discover an **exceptional match between your requirements for this opening and my skills and qualifications**:

Your Requirements:	My Qualifications:
Diploma in metal working	Diploma in Jewellery/Metalsmithing from XYZ School of Art, 20–.
Bench work/experience with jewellery repair practices	Jewellery repair and bench work for local retail jeweller: stone setting, soldering, pearl stringing, ring sizing, jewellery designing, and riveting. Valuation and maintenance.
Teaching, jewellery design education, and curriculum development	Two years' teaching experience. Comprehensive knowledge of casting gained through education, freelance and contract work includes wax carving, wax chasing, and mould making.
Excellent communication skills	Excellent oral and written self-expression. Give clear instructions and relate well to students. Relaxed communication style fosters encouragement and support. Subscribe to open-door policy.
Commitment to working with a diverse population	Successfully teach and interact with physically and mentally challenged individuals, as well as people of all ages from varied backgrounds and cultures.
Ability to manage projects and set specific objectives.	Extremely goal-orientated, giving particular attention to planning and follow-up for positive results. Experience coordinating special events such as art shows.

Besides these qualifications, I am an avid photographer, have an interest in gemology, and produce an average of one large art object a month. Personal qualities include a cheerful, energetic demeanour, positive attitude, dedication, self-sufficiency and creative/innovative idea generation. I am passionate about art, teaching, and mentoring, and enjoy the twofold return of the enthusiasm I bring to class.

My CV is attached for your review. Thank you for your time and consideration.

Yours sincerely,

Sarah Anne Steel
0123456 7890
Attachment: CV

E-mail response to newspaper job posting (assistant director of student accommodation)

From: Brenda Young [byoung@email.com]
To: Recipient's e-mail address
Cc:
Subject: Assistant Director of Student Accommodation

Re: Reference Code: TC-E-5556E2

Dear Recipient's Name,

In response to your ad for an Assistant Director of Student Accommodation advertised in Sunday's *Newsday*, I have attached my CV for your review. To illustrate my qualifications further, the following outlines the scope of my experience as it pertains to the position's requirements.

Your requirements	My qualifications
• Bachelor's degree or four years' experience in lieu of degree.	• Master's degree in Clinical Counselling • Eight years' combined experience in hall of residence administration and counselling capacities.
• Promote and develop educational programming and maintain extensive budget.	• Plan, develop and implement educational programmes, and manage an operational budget.
• Administration of three to five halls of residence housing approximately 1,000 students.	• Administration of halls of residence housing up to 500 students.
• Supervise, develop and evaluate three to five full-time halls of residence directors.	• Supervise, develop and evaluate 26 Resident Advisors with direct responsibility for four RAs and a Head Resident Advisor (HRA).
• Develop departmental policies and procedures, manage area office including rent, occupancy and facilities records.	• Direct all aspects of front desk management and facilities maintenance operations.
• Assist in the development and leadership of departmental committees, and serve as manager for student conduct cases.	• One year as chair of Committees and Organizations for the Student body.

Thank you for your review and consideration. I look forward to hearing from you soon.

Yours sincerely,

Brenda Young
0123456 7890
Attachment: CV

E-mail response to newspaper job posting (heavy equipment operator)

Relocating to Scotland, Jack wants to secure a position that could capitalize on his diverse range of skills.

From: Jack Crouther [jlcrouther@email.com]
To: Recipient's e-mail address
Cc:
Subject: Heavy Equipment Operator position

Dear Recipient's Name,

Please review the attached CV in application for your Heavy Equipment Operator position advertised in *The Times Journal*.

My diverse range of experience includes over 10 years' experience operating and maintaining heavy equipment. In my current position, I operate backhoes, loaders, lulls, Gallion cranes, Ditch Witch trenchers (large and walk-behind), fork lifts, street sweepers and bucket trucks. In addition, I supervise the troubleshooting, maintenance and repair of all of the department's equipment.

Of equal importance are my supervisory and leadership skills where I have managed multiple crews of up to 40 employees. Being extremely diligent, I have assumed responsibility for overseeing and monitoring various projects and issues that affect the daily operations, efficiency and profitability of the company. I am recognized by senior management for consistently completing projects on time and within budget.

Working in several trades during my career has developed my strong multitasking abilities which have proven to be an asset in my current position. Additional areas of experience include plumbing, irrigation, landscaping, electrical work, fibre optics and carpentry. In each of these areas, I have received training and have worked independently.

I would welcome the opportunity to meet you to determine the contributions I can make to your company.

Thank you for your consideration.

Yours sincerely,

Jack L Crouther
0123456 7890
Attachment: CV

E-mail response to online job posting (administrative secretary)

From: Your Name [Your e-mail address]
To: Recipient's e-mail address
Co:
Subject: I put out administrative fires

Dear Recipient's Name,

I was excited to see the announcement for an Administrative Secretary position with the Wessex Fire and Rescue Service, and believe I am an excellent candidate. After reading the job posting, I arranged for an informative tour from my uncle, James Kenderline, which confirmed my interest in the position.

Throughout my career I have demonstrated a strong work ethic as well as outstanding secretarial, administrative, reception, and records maintenance skills. I am meticulous with detail, can multitask effectively, and resolve problems in a fast-paced and deadline-driven environment. Among my professional accomplishments are:

- Concurrently handled full-time employment, managed rental properties, and completed Degree in English Literature while maintaining punctuality and low absenteeism.
- Assumed additional responsibilities proactively, and as requested, such as researching and writing a well-received full-page article for a client newsletter – with only 4 hours' notice.
- Consistently performed top-quality work in all positions held and contributed ideas that streamlined processes and optimized productivity.

Working for the Fire and Rescue Service would be an exciting and honorable position, and I think that upon reading my CV, you will find that my qualifications would be a great fit for this job.

I look forward to a personal meeting when we can discuss how my credentials and work ethic could contribute to your organization.

Sincerely,

Your Name
1234567 8910
Attachment: CV

E-mail response to online job posting (data centre engineer)

From: Your Name [Your e-mail address]
To: Recipient's e-mail address
Cc:
Subject: Storage, cloud, and data centre engineering issues

Dear Recipient's Name,

I am the Data Centre Engineer at a dedicated high-security site with 1300 enterprise servers for a global provider of secure financial message services. Your job posting on _____ for a Data Centre Engineer fits my qualifications, and I am writing to express my interest.

In my current position, I have maintained the hardware, software, and environment to ensure constant message flow availability at 99.999% for over ten years. Furthermore, I have maintained an incident-free 6-hour CTR contract with a £500K nonperformance penalty for the same period.

My responsibilities include:

- Lead storage engineer, managing schedules and workload of three rotating assistant engineers.
- Manage the integrity of a third-party site on behalf of XYZ.
- 1st point of contact for resolution of all issues and face of XYZ for a client with globally dispersed sites.
- Increased responsiveness while decreasing customer resolution time.
- Reduced overtime by 50%.
- Run the cleanest computer storage rooms in the country.

I have been trained by one of the world's leading technology companies to anticipate customer needs and deliver satisfaction with calm, professional consistency and technical competency. As much as anyone can in data centre management, I deliver peace of mind to the client, because I anticipate and pay attention to the details all day, every day.

I am accustomed to interacting at all levels of an organization and with clients throughout the technical and management hierarchies. Most notable are my strengths in facilitating cooperation among cross-functional teams, diverse corporate cultures, and globally dispersed work groups.

I have attached my CV to provide more information about my strengths and career achievements. I would welcome the opportunity to discuss storage, cloud, and data centre engineering issues with you. Can we talk?

Sincerely,

Your Name
1234567 8910
Attachment: CV

E-mail response to online job posting (operations manager)

From: Your Name [Your e-mail address]
To: Recipient's e-mail address
Cc:
Subject: Hi-Performance Operations Manager job posting

Dear Recipient's Name,

The job posting on CareerBuilder says you need an Operations Manager who can impact the bottom line. Adding a seasoned operations manager like me to your staff will increase productivity because 'no one has money to burn in a tough economy'.

The match between your needs and my talents is ideal. My strengths lie in managing the labour and manufacturing operations that design, build, install, and manage equipment for environmental and production improvements. I am a leader both by example and through effective management of individuals and teams.

My attached CV will identify a dozen projects (and their impact) that have been successfully implemented. The work performed under my direction has always come in at or below budget, and my teams always meet project deadlines.

The CV summarizes my qualifications and achievements. Because 'proven skills' are best verified in person, I look forward to our conversation and will call early next week to schedule our meeting. Thank you for taking the time to read my CV, and for your consideration.

Sincerely,

Your Name
12345 67890
Attachment: CV

E-mail response to online job posting (senior PR professional)

From: Your Name [Your e-mail address]
To: Recipient's e-mail address
Cc:
Subject: _____ consumer PR

Dear Recipient's Name,

As a high-tech PR professional with 15 years' technology experience, I possess both the proven skills and drive that you seek and _____ is known for. My specific experience includes:

Point of Strategic Counsel
Primary contact for creation, execution, and delivery of messaging and launch strategies for both companies and board-level executives. This has resulted in superb client-management skills at the highest levels, demonstrated by repeat business as loyal clients stay with me over the years.

Manage High-Level Influential Relations with Key Press
Having developed long-term relationships as well as forging critical new relationships with key media, I understand the importance of managing those relationships with integrity, respect, reliability, and discretion. This has enabled me to craft and place stories in hundreds of outlets ranging from _____ to _____ .

Coach Team and Account Staff
I learned over the years that a team is only as good as its leader. And, it's more rewarding to be on the winning team. I lead by example, believe in positive reinforcement and recognition, and keep team members focused on our client's goals and objectives: our ultimate prize.

The attached CV will give you further insight into my capabilities. I feel confident that a meeting would demonstrate that my hi-tech public relations expertise would be a worthy addition to your team. I look forward to speaking to you soon.

Regards,

Your Name
12345 678910
Attachment: CV

Direct approach to a potential employer (entry-level network admin)

Network administrator seeking entry-level opportunity highlights his certifications to emphasize recent professional development, a good idea when attempting a ground-floor position.

From: Andrew J Stells [ajstells@anyisp.com]
To: Recipient's e-mail address
Cc:
Subject: Entry-level Network Administrator

Dear Recipient's Name,

With my **MCP Certification**, and imminent **A++ Network Certification**, I am seeking an **entry-level Network Administrator** position. A brief highlight of the skills and values I would bring to your organization include:

- Knowledge of installation, configuration, troubleshooting and repair of sophisticated, state-of-the-art software and hardware.

- Analytical, research, troubleshooting, interpersonal and organizational skills developed through on-the-job training within an IT environment.

- Proven success in prioritizing time, completing projects and meeting deadlines under time-sensitive circumstances, achieving stellar results.

- An energetic, enthusiastic and 'people-driven' communication style.

I would welcome a personal interview to explore further the merging of my training and knowledge with your **IT** needs. My CV is attached, and I thank you for your consideration.

Yours faithfully,

ANDREW J STELLS
0123456 7890
Attachment: CV

Direct approach to a potential employer (entry-level librarian)

Helena, who emigrated from Poland, has completed her master's in library science and is looking for her first full-time position in her career field.

Helena Swenka

12345 678901   1 Any Street   helenaswen@anyserver.com
                             Anytown AA1 1AA

November 15, 20–

Mr Jeffery Devine, Library Division Director
ABC Library
111 Any Avenue
Anytown AA1 1AA

Dear Mr Devine,

Does your library anticipate the need for an **Entry-Level Research or Reference Librarian or Cataloguer?** With my recent MSc in Information and Library Management from a CILIP-accredited programme, as well as internship experience in the reference department of academic and business libraries, perhaps I can be of service.

My CV is enclosed for your review. You will find evidence of my librarianship training, library database and computer skills, and work history. What you will not immediately see on my CV are my character traits and achievements – allow me to list some of them for you that I believe are relevant:

✓ *Hard-working, determined achiever – I set my sights high, whether attaining a **degree** at University of London in a demanding **MSc Degree** programme, or responding to reference requests with a high level of customer service and promptness (within 1–3 hours).*

✓ *Information technology knowledge and fast learner – My references will attest to how quickly I assimilated knowledge of library databases, computer software and integrated library automation systems. With hands-on experience using **Voyager Module, AACR2r, LC classification scheme, MARC format, and OCLC,** as well as **Lexis-Nexis, Dow-Jones, Dialog Web, and Classic,** I have worked with diverse reference materials such as legal, business, genealogy documents, as well as periodicals.*

✓ *Proactive problem-solver and team player – Using my broad foreign language skills (Polish, Russian, Slovak, German, Latin) allowed me to problem-solve with confidence and correctly catalogue foreign language materials while serving a **reference library internship** with The Anytown County Library. As an **intern cataloguer,** I worked cooperatively with others in serial publication cataloguing and serial control, achieving high rates of daily production.*

Providing high-level customer service and efficiency is my goal in library services and support. My knowledge and practical use of internet resources and navigational tools, combined with my experience with library databases, affords you the opportunity to hire an entry-level library professional with proven librarianship success. May we meet soon to discuss your needs? I will call your office next week to arrange a mutually convenient appointment, if that is agreeable with you. My CV is enclosed, and I thank you for your time and consideration.

Yours sincerely,

Helena Swenka

Helena Swenka
Enclosure: CV

Direct approach to a potential employer (manager)

Concerned that his company is not doing well financially, William has decided to 'test the waters' for another position similar to those he has had in the past.

WILLIAM C KITE

1 Any Street   12345 678901
Anytown AA1 1AA   Wmckite@hotmail.com

12 December 20–

Mr Jacob Abernathy
Warehouse and Assembly Services
17 Industrial Way
Anytown AA1 1AA

Dear Mr Abernathy,

More than ever, good companies need proven performers who can get results in competitive industries and a tough economy, whether working independently or leading teams. If you are in need of a Warehouse Manager, Inventory Control Specialist, Production Manager or Assembly Order Fulfilment Supervisor, consider my track record:

✓ Efficiently scheduled assembly, material handlers and warehouse personnel, and closely monitored interplant transfers of raw materials from 20 warehouses. Assembly production and distribution procedures yielded high levels of productivity: 90 per cent on-time delivery, including emergency orders, of up to £1 million in SKUs per week. (Expediter/Production Dept. Scheduler, ABC Ltd)

✓ Developed cooperative relationships with field sales reps of major companies, such as ABC Ltd, DEF Healthcare, and XYZ, and served as liaison with in-house account executives and customer service reps at The GHI Group, to streamline receiving and shipping operations and upgrade quality control. (Warehouse Manager, The JKL Group)

✓ As final assembly and inspection member of four-person team, met heavy production schedule (35 to 60 complex, fabricated units per day) with 6 per cent or less error rate. (Order Fulfilment Clerk, ABC Ltd)

✓ Working as part of a team, created, tested, packaged and directed to shipping custom ship sets of complex hose assemblies, meeting deadlines 99-plus per cent of the time. Used quality assurance testing methods, including pressure testing of assembled units, to ensure highest level of customer satisfaction. (Hose Fabrication Technician, ABC Ltd)

I am confident I can deliver similar results for your company.

Page 1 of 2

William C Kite
Page 2 of 2

With well-rounded experience in assembly, expediting and scheduling, shipping and receiving, order fulfilment, customer service, sales, supervision and training, and a 15-year track record of meeting deadlines in demanding (even emergency) situations, I believe I have the proven skills that can benefit your company.

In addition, I realize it is hard-working and cooperative people who deliver results. My focus on teamwork and productivity has proven successful in my past assignments. I am confident I can convince you that I have the technical experience and knowledge that you need, as well as the intangible qualities – enthusiasm, strong work ethic, dedication and dependability – to get the job done.

May we meet soon to discuss your needs? I will contact your office next week to arrange a mutually convenient appointment, if that is agreeable with you. My CV is enclosed, and I thank you for your consideration.

Yours sincerely,

William C Kite

Enclosure: CV

Direct approach to a potential employer (mental health)

An applicant seeking to advance his career.

··**PETER A EDGEWATERS**

Dear Recipient's Name,

Throughout my career, I have held increasingly responsible positions within the Mental Health Care service, gaining extensive experience in working both with patients and in administrative functions. My particular areas of expertise are:

- Physical Medicine and Rehabilitation
- Adult Intervention
- Family Counselling
- Legal Issues
- Government Regulations
- Child Evaluation

My greatest strength lies in my ability to communicate with all types of people and different levels of professionals. Being able to work with patients, physicians, legal officers and family members has enabled me to be a highly effective therapist and an advocate for the patient and the patient's family. As an Administration official, I have been inducted into the intricacies of the Mental Health Service and have been able to gain a thorough understanding of the workings of various government agencies as they relate to mental health, including the Benefits Agency, Department of Health, Social Services and other entities.

I feel my knowledge and strengths would be best applied as a consultant or Mental Rehabilitation Therapist. Further, I desire to return to a more focused health care organization such as yours and would welcome an opportunity for an interview with you in person.

I look forward to speaking to you at your earliest convenience and appreciate your time in reviewing my credentials and qualifications. I am confident that my professional knowledge and strengths, combined with my dedication, work ethic and energy, will add measurable value to your organization. My CV is enclosed, and I thank you for your consideration.

Yours sincerely,

Peter A Edgewaters

PETER A EDGEWATERS

Enclosure: CV

···

1 Any Street • Anytown AA1 1AA • 12345 678901 • xxxx@msn.com

Direct approach to a potential employer (senior customer service specialist)

This candidate's most impressive qualifications are summarized in an eye-catching bulleted list.

From: Maria H Berretta [mhberretta@anyisp.com]
To: Recipient's e-mail address
Cc:
Subject: Senior Customer Service

Dear Recipient's Name,

Are you looking for a Senior Customer Service Specialist who is:

- A consistent top performer with a strong desire to get the job done?
- A team player able to achieve results through coordination with employees in all functional areas?
- An effective communicator with excellent writing, training and telephone skills?
- Able to learn quickly, analyse complex information and find solutions to problems?
- Organized, thorough and precise?

I have a bachelor's degree in business administration and seven years' experience in the insurance/financial industry, serving in diverse roles as customer relations advisor and calculations processor. I have consistently received the highest ratings in my branch despite the fact that the difficult cases frequently find their way to my desk. I also contribute to my team by putting in extra time to clear backlogs and by analysing existing procedures to devise more efficient methods of operation.

I believe that I can make a positive contribution to ABC Insurance Company and look forward to meeting you to discuss my capabilities in detail. Thank you for your time and consideration. My CV is attached for your review.

Yours sincerely,

Maria H Berretta
01234 567891
Attachment: CV

Direct approach to a potential employer (research professional)

Darrin is a data specialist working for the local government, compiling birth/death and census statistics. He wants to enter the private sector to do more consumer/ product research projects.

Darrin Wilson

MARKET RESEARCH ANALYST

Dear Recipient's Name,

As a research professional, I understand that success depends on a strong commitment to *customer satisfaction*. Executing the basics and using logic and reasoning to identify the strengths and weaknesses of alternative solutions, conclusions or approaches to problems are key to increasing performance and market share. I believe that my background and education reflect a commitment and ability to find solutions to these challenges. I developed excellent skills in **project coordination and the design and development of research projects** that increased the effectiveness of my organization.

I am considered an energetic, aggressive and innovative leader who is extremely client-oriented.

My position encompasses multiple tasks and responsibilities that include:

* examining and analysing statistical data to forecast future trends and to identify potential markets;
* designing and implementing new formats for logging and transferring information while working as part of a team researching data and statistics.

Thank you for your consideration. I approach my work with a strong sense of urgency, working well under pressure and change. I look forward to meeting you personally so that we may discuss how I can make a positive contribution to your organization. My CV is enclosed for your review.

Yours faithfully,

Darrin Wilson

Darrin Wilson

Enclosure: CV

---

1 Any Street • Anytown AA1 1AA • 12345 678901 • dWilson53@excite.com

Direct approach to a potential employer (personal trainer)

James wants to move into fitness training after a long and successful career in general management, sales and customer relationship management.

JAMES J HUTCHISEN
PO Box 901 ◆ Anytown AA1 1AA
12345 678901 ◆ jjhutch@hotmail.com

Dear Recipient's Name,

Reflecting on my professional sales and management experience within the marine industry, it is at this point in my career I am seeking to pursue a long-term personal and professional goal of a challenging opportunity as a **Personal Trainer/Strength Coach** within a health club, physical therapy and/or fitness centre. Let me briefly highlight the skills, values and contributions I will bring to your organization:

- **Certified Personal Trainer/Health Fitness Instructor at leading training centre.**

- Possess over 25 years' health club experience with most types of cardiovascular, plate and free-weight systems.

- Proven ability to plan and implement training programmes through experience as a Personal Trainer for a health club.

- Strong general management, sales, marketing and customer relationship management expertise developed through 16 years as an Owner/Operator of a marine business.

- Comprehensive experience in human relations, within the retail/service arena, has characterized me as considerate, dependable, honest, straightforward, hard-working and personable.

Since a CV can neither fully detail all my skills and accomplishments, nor predict my potential to your organization, I would welcome the opportunity to meet and discuss the possible merging of my talent and experience with your personal trainer needs.

Yours faithfully,

James J Hutchisen

JAMES J HUTCHISEN

Enclosure: CV

Direct approach to a potential employer (registered nurse)

This applicant moving out of the Navy has gained a great deal of experience with trauma treatment and crisis management.

From: Richard P Isaacs [rpisaacs@isp.com]
To: Recipient's e-mail address
Cc:
Subject: RN, emergency/post-op/medicinal/infectious disease/oncology/end-of-file/crisis

Dear Recipient's Name,

In anticipation of completing my naval service in April 20–, I am seeking a civilian position that will capitalize on my experience and training as a Registered Nurse. I believe that my clinical background and specialized training in emergency response and crisis management would make me an asset to your nursing staff. With this in mind, I have enclosed a CV for your review that outlines my credentials.

Some key points you may find relevant to a nursing position with your centre include:

- Caring for a broad range of patients, ranging from infants to senior citizens, and including post-operative, medical, infectious disease, oncology and end-of-life scenarios.

- Developing rapport with diverse cultural groups, both in clinical and social settings. The patients I have dealt with cut across the full spectrum of ethnic and socioeconomic strata, from enlisted personnel to officers and their dependents.

- Completing training and engaging in field exercises that have prepared me for disaster response in a civilian community.

I am confident that my dedication to caring for patients and capacity to function as an integral part of a treatment team would allow me to make a significant contribution to the health and well-being of your patients. Please contact me via phone or e-mail to discuss how I might fulfil your needs in a clinical nursing role.

Thank you for your time and consideration. I look forward to speaking to you soon.

Yours sincerely,

Richard P Isaacs, RN
01234 567891
Attachment: CV

Direct approach to a potential employer (entertainment industry)

This e-mail begins with an attention-grabbing opening followed by statements indicating that she understands the high-energy demands and realities of the entertainment industry. She ends the letter with a call to action.

From: Mary Manson [mmanson@email.com]
To: Recipient's e-mail address
Cc:
Subject: Entry-level Entertainment Industry

Dear Recipient's Name,

If your company is looking for a highly motivated recent graduate with a BA in Media Studies and work experience with production companies, who understands that you start at the bottom, then we should talk.

I offer a combination of creative talents and a strong work ethic as well as the following qualifications:

- BA in Media Studies from the University of London

- Hands-on experience directing, acting in and producing short independent and student films

- Realistic understanding of the demands of the entertainment industry, gained through internships for TV production company

- Operating knowledge of a variety of audio and video equipment

While my attached CV provides a brief overview of my background, I look forward to a personal meeting at which time we can discuss your needs and my qualifications in detail.

I will call you next week to arrange a meeting; in the meantime, you can contact me at the number below. Thank you in advance for your time and consideration.

Yours sincerely,

Mary Manson

Mary Manson
0123456 7891
Attachment: CV

Direct approach to a potential employer (management)

Scott's recent experience with his last employer focused on IT implementation and project management. He seeks to gain a project management position with an IT consulting firm where he can make use of both his technical expertise and his management skills.

From: Scott McFadden [samcfadden@email.com]
To: Recipient's e-mail address
Cc:
Subject: Senior Account Management

Dear Recipient's Name,

Capitalizing on a career that encompasses substantial IT project management experience and extensive sales/marketing experience, I am seeking a new professional challenge that will combine these skills in a senior account management, project management or technical leadership role. With this goal in mind, I have attached a CV that outlines my qualifications.

Some key points that you may find relevant:

- *Managing the technical deployment of six different releases of Cannon's SalesTeamX-pert sales force automation tool over the past three years.*

- *Ensuring that hardware platforms in the field are prepared to receive the latest release and resolving technical issues impacting end-user training for 6,000 users at 34 sites across the UK.*

- *Pre- and post-sales support to key account decision-makers at FTSE 100 companies, delivering logistics solutions for import and export.*

- *Hands-on experience providing desk-side support to end-users; configuring hardware and installing software in the field; and delivering training to end-users and IT specialists.*

I would enjoy discussing with you in person how my capabilities can match your needs, and will contact you soon to arrange an appropriate time for an initial meeting.

Thank you for your time and consideration. I look forward to speaking to you soon.

Yours sincerely,

Scott A McFadden
0123456 7891
Attachment: CV

Direct approach to a potential employer (radiation safety officer)

This highly skilled and highly educated physicist is applying for the post of Radiation Safety Officer, which is his boss's job, as the boss leaves for another opportunity. He is competing with highly qualified external candidates, and his best asset is his familiarity with the institution, based on existing experience.

Michael Z Ostrowski
1 Any Street/Anytown AA1 1AA/12345 678901
michaelzo@earthlink.com

12 January 20–

Mr Zachary P Emerson
University of London
111 Any Avenue
Anytown AA1 1AA

Dear Mr Emerson,

Please accept this letter and the enclosed CV as an expression of my interest in the Radiation Safety Officer position you are currently seeking to fill. I am confident that my education, experience and familiarity with the University of London Research Centre facilities provide me with the necessary skills to meet or exceed your expectations in this role.

For the past year, I have been a Health Physicist with the university, with responsibility for a variety of functions, including:

- Testing & Monitoring Equipment
- Training Medical Staff
- Ensuring Compliance with Regulations
- Monitoring Staff Exposure
- Achieving CRESO Certification
- Supervising Four Technicians
- Serving on Various Committees
- Consulting with Physicians
- Maintaining Updated Technical Knowledge

Earlier, I held a similar position at University of Wales' School of Medicine and Hospital. There I trained and supervised the work of a six-person technical team. I ensured that all equipment, materials and supplies were in compliance with state regulations. State inspection results were always outstanding. Throughout my career, I have built a reputation for quality, flexibility and professionalism in all areas. My commitment to health and safety has resulted in a perfect safety record.

I hold two master's degrees, one in Nuclear Engineering from City University, the other in Nuclear Physics from South West University. I have taught Biophysics at university level. In addition, I speak three languages (English, Portuguese and Russian). Having lived and worked in other countries has given me a sensitivity and understanding of diverse cultures and customs.

I have thoroughly enjoyed working at the university, and would welcome this opportunity to make an even more significant contribution to the success of its mission. I would enjoy discussing my qualifications with you in person and invite you to contact me to arrange an initial interview.

Thank you for your time and consideration. I look forward to speaking to you soon.

Yours sincerely,

Michael Z Ostrowski

Michael Z Ostrowski
Enclosure: CV

Direct approach to a potential employer (veterinary surgeon)

This veterinary surgeon practises in an elite niche, treating only competitive horses at race courses.

From: Parker Douglass [pdouglass@email.com]
To: Recipient's e-mail address
Cc:
Subject: Veterinary Surgeon

Dear Recipient's Name,

My 15 years' experience addressing the health and performance needs of elite race horses at major tracks makes me a strong candidate for the opening you recently advertised on your website. Accordingly, I have attached my CV for your consideration and review.

Some key points include:

- **Strong capacity to function independently and make critical decisions without direct supervision. My knowledge of horses and experience at several major race courses means that I will need minimal orientation to 'hit the ground running'.**
- **An excellent track record of maintaining the health of elite thoroughbreds and quarter horses, as well as assisting trainers in enhancing the performance of horses by improving their respiratory and general health as well as dealing with lameness issues (references can be provided).**
- **The ability to effectively evaluate young horses prior to purchase, through observation and diagnostic testing. I routinely produce quality repository radiographs and review radiographs in a repository setting. I also accompany buyers to auctions to assess horses being considered.**
- **Experience assisting trainers setting up effective farm-based training programmes, as well as helping breeders address reproductive health issues.**

I believe that I can be an asset to your organization and would enjoy discussing further how my knowledge, expertise and professional dedication can address your needs. Please feel free to contact me to arrange either a phone or in-person interview at a mutually convenient date and time.

Thank you for your time and consideration. I look forward to speaking to you soon.
My CV is attached for your review.

Yours sincerely

Parker Douglass
0123456 7890
Attachment: CV

Direct approach to a potential employer (internship)

This is a cover letter to apply for a competitive internship in the financial services industry.

Carlos M Nunez

13 January 20–

Current Address
City University
1 Any Street
Anytown AA1 1AA

Telephone: 12345 678901
Email: nunezc@cu.edu

Permanent Address
111 Any Road
Anothertown BB1 1BB

Telephone: 10987 654321

Karen Carmichael
XYZ Ltd
111 Any Avenue
Anytown AA1 1AA
Re: Finance Intern

Dear Ms Carmichael:

Are you looking for a driven, high-achieving intern committed to excelling in business and finance?

As a student at City University, I am pursuing a BA in Business Administration with an emphasis on Finance. My passion for financial markets and economics has steadily increased over the last five years and I am committed to developing my career path as a business leader within a major organization.

I approach all my work with discipline and focus; as an intern with your organization, I would look forward to effectively contributing to your programme goals. City University, ABC Academy, and The ABC Club of London have acknowledged my academic and leadership achievements for excellence in academic studies, volunteering, and peer mentoring.

Please feel free to contact me at my number in London, 12345 678901. Thank you for your consideration. I am enthusiastic about working at XYZ Ltd. My background, professionalism and enthusiasm will make me an effective member of your team.

Yours sincerely,

Carlos M Nunez

Enclosure: CV

Direct approach to a potential employer (teacher)

A cover letter sent with the CV hard copy as a follow-up to the CV submission via e-mail.

.... **JONATHAN YOUNG**

14 November 20–

Ms Jennifer Jones
Personnel Coordinator
ABC Language School
111 Any Avenue
Anytown AA1 1AA

Dear Ms Jones,

Although I recently submitted my CV to your office via e-mail, I am submitting the enclosed hard copy as a follow-up. I welcome any questions you might have.

With this letter, I would like to reiterate my sincere motivation to teach in Japan. My experience as a substitute middle school teacher has helped me to understand methods of student interaction and reach a level of comfort in the classroom. I strive to build relationships with students – as much as a substitute teacher can – to facilitate classroom activities and inspire the learners. It is something I really enjoy.

The ABC website encourages 'all outgoing, dynamic, and flexible people to apply'. In my current position as a flight attendant for XYZ Airlines, I am required to demonstrate these characteristics daily. Communication and quick-thinking skills are a must onboard an aircraft full of passengers. Flexibility is essential in the areas of customer service, in interaction with colleagues, and in work scheduling.

My motivation is indeed genuine, and I look forward to the possibility of discussing the opportunity with you. I will gladly make myself available for a telephone or videoconference interview.

Yours sincerely,

Jonathan Young

Jonathan Young

Enclosure: One-page CV

---

1 Any Street • Anytown AA1 1AA • 12345 678901 • jon@jonyoung.com

Direct approach to a potential employer (production supervisor)

Two problems to overcome: a move from automotive service manager to production supervisor and a break in employment of more than a year.

FERGUS McLEAN
        1 Any Street
        Anytown AA1 1AA

        12345 678901
        FML5505@anyserver.co.uk

Tuesday, 28 October 20–

Mr Charles W Worth
Director of Operations
ABC Ltd
111 Any Avenue
Anytown AA1 1AA

Dear Mr Worth,

How big is that gap between what the ABC leadership wants from its skilled, semi-skilled and unskilled employees and what the ABC bottom line gets? If you'd like to shrink that costly mismatch, we should explore adding me to your team as your Transportation Manager.

On the next pages, you'll see more than a half-dozen contributions I have made in this area. They illustrate the five profit-building capabilities I've listed right at the top of the next page. I'd like to put those advantages to work for you right away.

Over the last year, the health of a family member made the most demands upon me and guided my relocation from Anytown to Anothertown. Now that problem is resolved and I am ready to return to my first love: helping teams want to do well.

If my approach and philosophy appeal to you, please let me suggest a next step. I would like to hear about your specific needs in your own words. May I call in a few days to arrange a time to do that?

Yours sincerely,

Fergus McLean

Fergus McLean

Enclosure: CV

Direct approach to a potential employer (sales professional)

George has two specific needs: to show the sales aspect of his previous career as an accountant, and to convince a new employer that his desire to leave his current company was based solely upon having to work in an oversold market.

From: George Williams [gwilliams@email.com]
To: Recipient's e-mail address
Cc:
Subject: Sales

Dear Recipient's Name,

I want you to get the credit for adding ROI to the XYZ sales team. Specifically, I'd like to become your newest sales professional. Perhaps the best way to link those two ideas is with a CV that shows how I'm performing right now.

What I do isn't magic. I just work harder and smarter than my competition by finding some profitable way to say yes to every customer and potential customer.

In my attached CV, I believe you will see something that offers more than the usual recitations of job titles and responsibilities. That's why you'll find six capabilities I want to put at XYZ's disposal at once. Backing them up are a dozen examples of sales that show those capabilities in action.

My company values what I do. And, if I thought our market was growing as fast as yours, I would stay with them. While I cannot control market conditions, I am interested in making even greater contributions to my employer. That's why I'm 'testing the waters' with this confidential application.

I do best using the consultative approach to sales. So, as a first step, I'd like to hear about XYZ's sales needs in your own words. May I call in a few days to arrange a time to do that?

Yours sincerely,

George Williams
0123456 7890
Attachment: CV

Direct approach to a potential employer (credit account specialist)

Kim wants to affiliate herself with a larger company that offers a more challenging role in analysing and managing financial accounts; she also seeks to take on more responsibility to allow her to grow professionally.

From: Kimberly Carter [kcarter@email.com]
To: Recipient's e-mail address
Cc:
Subject: Credit/Collections

Dear Recipient's Name,

I bring over 18 years of accounts receivable experience in addition to being involved in all processing stages of collections, resolving payment issues, and collecting on past-due payments. The scope of my experience includes, but is not limited to, commercial, automotive and manufacturing environments.

I focus on delivering results and providing superior service by quickly identifying problem areas in accounts receivable and developing a solution strategy to ensure issues are resolved. My expertise lies in my strong ability to build rapport with clients, analyse accounts, and manage all aspects related to my appointed position and areas of responsibility.

Due to circumstances beyond my control, I was unable to continue my employment as a cash applications analyst with a well-known automotive industry leader. My objective is to secure a position in accounts receivable and credit collections with an established company.

My attached CV details my skills, experience, and the contributions I have made to employers. I look forward to speaking to you soon to answer any questions you may have regarding my background and I will follow up this e-mail with a phone-call next week.

Yours sincerely,

Kimberly Carter
0123456 7890
Attachment: CV

Direct approach to a potential employer (sales)

After 'playing around' with part-time and seasonal positions for six years after college, John was ready to combine his variety of sales and customer service achievements into a bid for a serious, high-paying sales career.

From.   John Anderson [jmanderson@omail.com]
To: Recipient's e-mail address
Cc:
Subject: Sales

Dear Recipient's Name,

My first job in sales management was straight out of college, running a beach bar. My competitors were like flies – they kept popping up everywhere, opening with lots of glitz, taking all the customers, and then crashing and burning after six months. But during those six months they were trying to take all _my_ customers! These were serious challenges to which I responded with all the best tactics I could muster – free pool playing, fruity drinks for girls; sports TV; I even gave away free beer one night.

Today I am the same aggressive, ambitious sales professional I was then. OK… these days I wouldn't give away free beer, but I _do_ respond to sales challenges with all the competitiveness, creativity and customer concern in my heart. In my last sales position, I was quite successful selling holiday packages by telephone for several reasons:

- I qualified my targets well.
- I was very knowledgeable about the product and painted a good picture of the product in the customer's mind.
- I think well and profitably on my feet.
- I'm honest and a natural rapport-builder.

The point of my attached CV is that I would like to talk to you about putting all my sales, problem-solving and customer service skills to work for your organization. When can we meet? My CV is attached for your review.

Yours sincerely,

John Michael Anderson
0123456 7890
Attachment: CV

Direct approach to a potential employer (media)

Letting her professors speak for her and then confirming their words with her own words of commitment is a very effective strategy. The strength of the text is enhanced by the brevity of the letter.

BROOKE M WELLINGTON   brookewelli@anyserver.co.uk

1 Any Street ◆ Anytown AA1 1AA ◆ Phone: 12345 678901

'I would rank Ms Wellington's work in the top 10 per cent of students I have taught; she is not afraid to tackle tough projects; I believe she has the ability to make positive contributions…'

– John Weiss, PhD, Chairperson, Department of Communications, City College

'Brooke was an exemplary Journalism student. She took charge of the tasks given to her and performed them in a superior manner. I admire her strong enthusiasm and her attention to detail…'

– Stephen M Ross, Assistant Director of Television Technical Operations, City College

---

Dear Selection Committee,

Tenacious and *driven* are terms my colleagues have used to describe my work habits. It is with a strong sense of career commitment that I submit my CV for your review.

Having completed classes in August, I will be granted a BA in Journalism from City College in December 20–. Sometimes holding two jobs while attending college, I will have completed my degree in three years. It is with the same passion, integrity and energy that I intend to pursue my career.

Like so many, I possess the talent and understanding of how demanding a career in media can be. But unlike most, I am willing to 'pay the price' of hard work, demanding work schedules and total availability that the industry requires.

Thanks so much for your consideration. I am eager to learn more about the challenges facing your organization and to discuss how I can make a difference.

Yours sincerely,

Brooke M Wellington

Brooke M Wellington
Enclosure: CV

Direct approach to a potential employer (director)

From: Richard Carpenter [rcarpenter@email.com]
To: Recipient's e-mail address
Cc:
Subject: CFO, global and boardroom performer

Dear Recipient's Name,

As a Chief Financial Officer, I have built a reputation for strategic business and financial planning for global organizations. My ability to identify challenges and to capitalize upon opportunities to expand revenue growth, reduce operating costs and improve overall productivity has been one of my strongest assets.

My strengths in financial and accounting management as well as my thorough understanding of finance operations have vastly contributed to my career and success as a leader. I maintain self-confidence, credibility and stature to make things happen with colleagues. Just as significant are my abilities to develop rapport among co-workers and management, build effective teams and promote team effort.

My objective is to secure a position as a CFO or Director and to pursue new opportunities with an organization providing new and exciting challenges. Having a complete picture of my expertise and experience is very important. As you will note in my CV, I have made significant contributions to my employers and take my job very seriously.

I appreciate your time and consideration and will be in contact next week to see if we are able to arrange a date for an interview. I look forward to speaking to you soon. My CV is attached for your review.

Yours sincerely,

Richard Carpenter
0123456 78901
Attachment: CV

Direct approach to a potential employer (career change to pharmaceutical sales)

From: Elana Carter [ecarter@email.com]
To: Recipient's e-mail address
Cc:
Subject: Pharmaceutical Sales

Dear Recipient's Name,

I currently hold a sales management position for a very successful retail company. My talents to achieve high sales volume, work cooperatively with diverse personalities, and focus on providing exceptional customer service have allowed me to excel in customer relations and succeed in sales and marketing.

I want to extend my experience into the field of pharmaceutical sales. I thoroughly understand the importance of developing customer relations, generating revenue from sales potential within a designated territory, and maintaining accurate customer information. Pharmaceutical sales has been an interest of mine for some time, and I am confident that my background will allow me to make the transition without difficulty.

I have the aptitude and willingness to learn the necessary technical medical materials to promote your products. What I may lack in specific experience in your business, I more than make up for with my dedication, energy and determination.

Your time in reviewing my attached, confidential CV is greatly appreciated. I will follow up next week to answer any questions you may have regarding my qualifications. At that time, I would like to discuss the possibility of setting up a personal interview with you. Please contact me if you would like to speak sooner.

Yours sincerely,

Elana Carter
012345 67890
Attachment: CV

Direct approach to a potential employer (recruiter)

Interested in fast-track career progression, Betsy has reached her peak with her current employer. She is seeking a position in a high-growth global company.

BETSY McGILL

1 Any Street • Anytown AA1 1AA • 12345 678901

(Date)

Alice _____
(Title)
A, B&C
Executive Search Consultants
111 Any Avenue
Anytown AA1 1AA

Dear Ms _____,

Having spent several years in executive recruitment, I understand the number of CVs you receive on a daily basis. However, I remember how valuable a few always turned out to be.

The purpose of this communication is to introduce myself and then to meet you with a view to joining your organization.

When asked which business situations have been the most challenging and rewarding, my answer is the time spent in the search profession.

My background, skills and talents are in all aspects of sales and sales management. My research indicates that your expertise is in this area.

I have enclosed a CV that will highlight and support my objectives. I would appreciate the opportunity to meet you and exchange ideas. I will call you over the next few days to make an appointment. If you prefer, you may reach me in the evening or leave a message at 12345 678901.

Thank you and I look forward to our meeting.

Yours sincerely,

Betsy McGill

Betsy McGill

Enclosure: CV

Direct approach to a potential employer (project management)

From: Matthew Sims [msims@email.com]
To: Recipient's e-mail address
Cc:
Subject: IT Project Manager

Dear Recipient's Name,

Information technology expertise, combined with leadership, the ability to motivate cross-functional teams, and develop cost-effective solutions, are key to creating long-term customer satisfaction and loyalty.

As a seasoned **Project Manager** experienced in providing strategic direction in the design and deployment of technology solutions, I have:

- successfully managed customer accounts from defining project requirements through to implementation;
- engineered e-commerce business solutions for myriad organizations from start-up ventures to FTSE 100 companies;
- completed all the coursework, including specialized electives, to obtain the Microsoft Certified Systems Engineer designation;
- developed comprehensive RFIs and RFPs; selected the most qualified, cost-effective vendor; and directed cross-functional teams to ensure on-time, on-budget implementation;
- efficiently prioritized projects, developed realistic timelines and consistently met deadlines;
- compiled and driven ratification of product requirements;
- provided technical expertise to sales teams to assist them in closing the sale.

Could your company use a high achiever with a thirst for growth and new challenges? If so, I would like to discuss how my skills and experience could benefit your organization. I have attached my CV for your consideration, and I look forward to speaking to you.

Yours sincerely,

Matthew Sims
0123456 7890
Attachment: CV

Direct approach to a potential employer (publishing)

An administrative support person who wants to break into the publishing industry. She has no actual experience but is an avid reader who volunteers time to edit community fundraising publications and newsletters.

From: Genevieve Stone [gstone@email.com]
To: Recipient's e-mail address
Cc:
Subject: PA publishing

Dear Recipient's Name,

In the interest of exploring opportunities in the publishing industry, I have enclosed my CV for your review. Over the last two years, I have gained valuable knowledge and experience in many aspects of personnel assistance, office procedures and administrative operations.

Recently I volunteered my time to edit a cookbook and have been responsible for editing the newsletter for my college. I consider myself a good writer and an avid reader and have always wanted to get into publishing.

With my considerable energy, drive and ability to work long hours, I believe I could make a positive contribution to your organization, and I would appreciate the opportunity to discuss my qualifications with you.

Thank you for your time and consideration. I look forward to meeting you. My CV is attached for your review.

Yours sincerely,

Genevieve Stone
01234 567890
Attachment: CV

Direct approach to a potential employer (international sales)

·· **JENNIFER DELOREAN**

(Date)

Phillip _____
(Title)
ABC Ltd
1 Industry Plaza
Anytown AA1 1AA

Dear Mr _____,

I received your name from Mr _____ last week. I spoke to him regarding career opportunities with _____ and he suggested contacting you. He assured me that he would pass my CV along to you; however, in the event that he did not, I am enclosing another.

As an avid cosmetics consumer, I understand and appreciate the high standards of quality that your firm honours. As you can see from my enclosed CV, I have had quite a bit of experience in the international arena. My past experience working overseas has brought me a greater understanding of international cultures and traditions, as well as a better understanding and appreciation of our own culture. These insights would certainly benefit a company with worldwide locations, such as your own. In addition, I have gained first hand experience in the consumer marketplace through my various sales positions. I have noticed your recent expansion into the television media and am sure that an energetic individual would surely be an asset to ABC in this, as well as other, projects.

I would very much like to discuss career opportunities with ABC. I will be calling you within the next few days to set up an interview. In the meantime, if you have any questions I may be reached at the number above. Thank you for your consideration.

Yours sincerely,

Jennifer Delorean

Jennifer Delorean

Enclosure: CV

··
1 Any Street • Anytown AA1 1AA • 12345 678901
internationalsalespro@msn.com

Direct approach to a potential employer (banking)

Having completed a one-year contract, Matthew had been offered a permanent position. However, he is interested in a position in a company that is more financially stable, and one where he could make use of his diverse technology skills.

From: Matthew Lorenzo [bankerpro@hotmail.com]
To: Recipient's e-mail address
Cc:
Subject: Financial management / Sales orientation

Dear Recipient's Name,

Please include my name in your job search database. As requested, I have attached a copy of my current CV.

Banking today is definitely a sales environment. While my marketing skills will always be useful, my interests lead me now to seek a more distinct financial management position such as Controller, Treasurer, or Head of Finance.

Since my CIMA Part III will be completed in January 20–, my search may be somewhat premature, but my transcript and results, combined with my practical experience, should offset my temporary lack of an accounting designation. I would therefore like you to begin considering me immediately. As an Account Manager, I saw many different industries, and so would not feel constrained to any one sector.

Including a mortgage loan benefit, I am currently earning £4,500 per month plus a car allowance. This should provide you with an indication of my present job level. Your suggestions or comments would be appreciated. I am available for interviews, and can be reached at 12345 678901. Thank you.

Yours sincerely,

Matthew Lorenzo
012345 678901
Attachment: CV

Direct approach to a potential employer (software development)

From: Julie Baxter [softwarespecialist@anyserver.co.uk]
To: Recipient's e-mail address
Cc:
Subject: Developer with quality, productivity and commitment

Dear Recipient's Name,

ABC Ltd caught my attention recently as I began a search for a new employer in the South West area. ABC Ltd is well known in the software industry for quality products and excellent customer service; it also maintains a strong reputation as a great employer. Your organization has created an environment in which people can excel, which is why I write to you today.

I am very interested in joining your software development team. I am confident that my background and experience will meet your future needs. My current position is Application Developer for XYZ Ltd. I enjoy it very much as it has provided me with extensive hands-on training in Visual Basic and other languages. However, I am ready to get more into actual software writing, as well as return to the Bristol area. I possess a bachelor's degree in Computer Science as well as training in a variety of programming languages. I am also a fast learner, as demonstrated by my learning Visual Basic quickly after joining XYZ. Additionally, I plan to pursue my master's degree and have begun the application process.

I would appreciate the opportunity to meet you to discuss your goals and how I can help you meet them. I will call you soon to arrange a meeting. In the meantime, please feel free to call for further information on my background and experience.

Thank you for your consideration and reply. I look forward to meeting you in the near future.

Yours sincerely,

Julie Baxter
12345 678901
Attachment: CV

Direct approach to a potential employer (internship)

From: David Kent [internationalrelationspro@earthlink.net]
To: Recipient's e-mail address
Cc:
Subject: Motivated International Relations Intern

Dear Recipient's Name,

I am interested in being considered for an internship. I am currently in my final year at the University of XYZ studying International Studies with a concentration on Latin America and Political Science.

Previous internships have increased my knowledge of International Relations and have enabled me to make use of my education in a professional environment. I am very serious about my International Relations education and future career and am eager to learn as much as possible throughout my internship. I am interested in working for your organization to gain practical experience and additional knowledge pertaining to my field of study.

My professional and academic background, along with my sincere interest in helping others, has enhanced my sensitivity to a diverse range of cultures. As a highly motivated professional, I enjoy the challenge of complex demanding assignments. My well-developed writing and communication skills are assets to an office environment.

I welcome the opportunity to elaborate on how I could make a substantial contribution to your organization as an intern. I look forward to talking to you soon. Thank you.

Yours sincerely,

David Kent
12345 678901
Attachment: CV

Direct approach to a potential employer (financial planning professional)

The employer was so impressed with the detail of the cover letter that he offered a position to this applicant at the initial interview.

David Meyers
1 Any Street ▪ Anytown AA1 1AA
Phone: 12345 678910 ▪ Mobile: 1098765 4321 ▪ E-mail: meyerstown@juno.com

19 September 20–

David Borgrum
ABC Financial Manager
111 Any Avenue
Anytown AA1 1AA

Dear Mr Borgrum,

The Rock. ABC is known internationally by this symbol of security and permanence, the assurance to their clients the company will always be there. The corporate slogan 'Increasing and Protecting Your Wealth' can only be sustained through principled management, effective investment strategies and ethical financial planning. I am a financial planner who strictly adheres to these same principles.

My qualifications include:

- Registered Investment Advisor.
- BA in Economics.
- Commitment to client satisfaction and quality service through needs assessments.
- Demonstrated results in business development and execution of marketing strategies.
- Effective communication and presentation skills necessary to articulate product benefits clearly and accurately to clients.
- Outstanding time management and organizational ability.
- A willingness to 'go the extra mile' for client and corporation.

Furthermore, I am skilled at new business development, cold calling and seminar presentations. Employers and colleagues have consistently praised my attention to detail, strong work ethic and ability to deal with the most complex client engagements.

Please contact me at your earliest convenience to set up an interview concerning employment opportunities within your company. I look forward to hearing from you.

Yours sincerely,

David Meyers

David Meyers

Direct approach to a potential employer (chef/hotel/restaurant manager)

Michael started as a chef and went into the management side of the restaurant. He is now hoping to work for a multi-restaurant chain in a management capacity.

Michael J Fisher

1 Any Street
Anytown AA1 1AA
12345 678910

Dear Recipient's Name,

I am confident that my 23 years' experience as a chef and hotel/restaurant manager would be an asset to your organization.

I am currently General Manager and Corporate Executive Chef of ABC London. In 20–, I was hired to start up this 225-seat restaurant and be responsible for all financial reporting and key control systems to meet the standards of the parent company XYZ. Achievements include gaining excellent media publicity, creative menu development, directing on- and off-site catering for many city events, and coordinating all aspects of construction and design of our new kitchen.

As Director of Operations for DEF Catering and the DEF Restaurant in Oxford, my staff and I expanded the business to accommodate parties ranging from 10 to 4,000 people and grossed over £1.5 million in sales.

Working as Director of Operations and Executive Chef for JKL Hotels, I oversaw all profit and loss functions for a 165-seat à la carte restaurant and a 1,000-seat banquet facility. The hotel had an 18-hole Championship Golf Course that I managed, with an active membership of 1,000 members.

I gained extensive international experience working as Executive Chef for MNO, a five-star-rated restaurant in New Zealand. I prepared food for the Prime Minister, various heads of state, and visiting dignitaries. I obtained my New Zealand Master Chef's Certification. In addition, I served as an Executive Pastry Chef and Chef for a Hawaiian hotel owned and operated by the Sheraton Corporation.

Thank you for your consideration. I look forward to speaking to you personally regarding my qualifications and how I can contribute positively as a member of your management staff.

Yours faithfully,

Michael J Fisher

Michael J Fisher

Direct approach to a potential employer (maintenance mechanic)

Elizabeth was a bus driver who changed to a warehouse position, and eventually to a higher-paying maintenance mechanic position. After redundancy, she wishes to continue her career as a mechanic.

From: Elizabeth Denton [edenton@email.com]
To: Recipient's e-mail address
Cc:
Subject: Maintenance Mechanic

Dear Recipient's Name,

As a **Facilities** and **Maintenance Mechanic** with 16 years' experience, I understand that the timely maintenance and repair of machinery, supervision of maintenance programmes, and monitoring outside contractors have a real impact on company reputation and success.

Throughout my career I have been promoted and have successfully assumed increasing responsibilities. In my latest position as a Mechanic for ABC Foods, I had the reputation for excellent machinery knowledge and a keen attention to detail.

ABC Foods is downsizing the factory in Anytown, and I have accepted voluntary redundancy from the company. I would like to continue my career with a new company offering me new challenges.

Thank you for your consideration. I possess excellent hands-on knowledge as well as supervisory expertise, and I look forward to meeting you personally so that we can discuss how I can make a positive contribution to your team.

Yours sincerely,

Elizabeth Denton
0123456 7890
Attachment: CV

Direct approach to a potential employer (database engineer)

Edward Kumamoto
kumamotoed@islandnet.com

1 Any Street
Anytown AA1 1AA

Home: 12345 687910
Mobile: 1098765 4321

(Date)
Phillip _____
(Title)
ABC Ltd
1 Industry Plaza
Anytown AA1 1AA

Dear Mr _____,

Empowering your employees with the information and tools necessary to make better strategic business decisions is very likely to improve your company's competitive advantage and profitability. I can do this through insightful strategic planning and the delivery of superior data warehouse and decision support systems.

My extensive career experience in data warehousing, database administration and business systems development, coupled with my commitment to exceed customer expectations and my focus on achieving sustainable strategic competitive advantage, are the primary assets I would bring to your Director of Database Engineering position. I have successfully delivered numerous data warehouse projects that were effectively aligned with company strategic objectives. I am also highly skilled at directing teams on complex initiatives and improving processes, communication, teamwork and quality.

As a senior-level employee of Information Technology Ltd, I have established an excellent track record of successfully managing large complex projects. Notably, I managed a £10 million development project for XYZ Ltd, building and implementing their first enterprise data warehouse and certain downstream divisional data marts. So successful was this project that within three months of implementation it established itself as the recognized supreme source of accurate company data for all of XYZ's business units. Additionally, it met tight service level commitments over 97 per cent of the time and experienced no downtime due to programming error.

As a Project Leader/Manager for DEF Business Systems, I also managed the development of a large data warehouse. I led the design and development efforts for this data warehouse of sales information for their Speciality Products division. This was the first data warehouse developed at DEF that successfully met user expectations.

An additional asset I would bring to your organization is competency in correlating data warehousing functions with overall company goals. I am skilled in providing counsel to senior managers and executives and adept at monitoring data warehouse systems to ensure their value and usefulness to an organization as a whole.

I am confident that this experience equips me for success as your Director of Database Engineering. Kindly review my CV, then please contact me at your earliest convenience to arrange a professional interview.

Yours sincerely,

Edward Kumamoto
Enclosure: CV

Direct approach to a potential employer (senior technical sales)

From: Stephanie Newman [snewman@email.com]
To: Recipient's e-mail address
Cc:
Subject: Technical Sales

Dear Recipient's Name,

As a seasoned Technical Services and Marketing Associate, I've generated considerable new business for my previous employers, and now I'd like to do the same for you. For the past 15 years I have pursued an increasingly successful career in telecommunications sales and marketing. Among my accomplishments are:

SALES
Competent with the entire sales management process, from initial client consultation and needs assessment through to product demonstration, price and service negotiations, and final sales closings. Sales increased 23 per cent over last five years.

MARKETING
Success in orchestrating all aspects of marketing strategy, from competitive market intelligence and trend analysis, product development, launch and positioning to distribution management and customer care.

TELECOMMUNICATIONS & NETWORK SOLUTIONS
Recognized for pioneering technology solutions that meet the needs of complex customer service, logistics, and distribution operations. Able to test operations to ensure optimum systems functionality and availability, guide systems implementation across multiple platforms and deliver user training and support programmes that outpace the competition.

Please see my attached CV. I look forward to learning about any available opportunities in your organization.

Yours sincerely,

Stephanie Newman
0123456 7890
Attachment: CV

Direct approach to a potential employer (telecommunications)

Tom Clancy
1 Any Street • Anytown AA1 1AA • telecompro@anyserver.co.uk
Home: 12345 678901 • Work: 55555 555555 • Mobile: 1098765 4321

(Date)

Emily _____
(Title)
ABC Ltd
1 Industry Plaza
Anytown AA1 1AA

Dear Ms _____,

If you need someone with proven international success who will really listen to your clients' needs and has leaped over cultural barriers to forge some of the most profitable technical opportunities in the telecommunications field, I am your number 1 choice for any opportunity in international or domestic sales or marketing.

For the last 10 years, my work in strategic partnering, developing alliances, creating new opportunities and exceeding multinational clients' expectations has helped my employers to more than double their sales. However, follow-up, tenacious attention to detail, and my ability to listen have solidified longstanding relationships with major players worldwide.

With a global leader in telecommunications, I received three promotions in four years due to my success in managing contacts, motivating staff and implementing marketing campaigns that delivered ROI threefold.

Since 20, I have:

- Marketed a full range of data and voice communication services to multinational corporations and Internet service providers in Japan, Southeast Asia, Canada and Western Europe.
- Brought in 28 new global accounts representing up to a 250 per cent increase in business – currently handle brand management efforts for XYZ on track to exceed annual goal; managed 20 accounts requiring broadband connectivity to international locations.
- Created the first transcontinental ATM circuit and earned one of the most prestigious awards in the company.
- Trained technical associates in ATM and employed knowledge of DWDM, SONET, SDMS, and TCP/IP technology to create some of the most cost-effective networks on the planet.

Page 1 of 2

Tom Clancy
Page 2 of 2

If these proven successes sound like the work of a go-getter you need on board:

- Consider that, in just two years with a system software developer, I added £1.5m in new business, trained an all-Japanese staff in direct marketing principles, and launched direct sales campaigns that increased client awareness of our services.

Additionally, my efforts with an international contractor:

- Partnered the parent company with Japan-based joint venture interests that enabled the first UK-built airport in Japan.
- Kept Japanese executives and high-ranking government officials apprised of progress – and landed two additional opportunities for a total of £10m in business in just a year.

Technically speaking:

- I have worked with ATM, Frame Relay, Private Line, SONET, DWDM, SNA/SDLE, SDMS, and IP, and managed networks and a diverse array of hardware and software packages – in addition to holding numerous Novell and Windows specialized certifications.

I love calling on clients who have been let down by other reps, because I know my negotiating skills, ability to cross cultural barriers and generate win–win opportunities will get the decision-maker to sign every time.

Reviewing my attached CV, you will note doctoral, master's and bachelor's degrees – and a host of quantifiable results and technical training that serve only to enhance my drive and enthusiasm. I will gladly set aside time to meet you and discuss how my knowledge of technology, client relations and strategic partnering can become your biggest asset.

I will take the liberty of contacting you on Monday at 10 am. If you need to reach me, please feel free to contact me at 12345 678901. Thanking you in advance for the opportunity to meet you,

Yours sincerely,

Tom Clancy

Tom Clancy

Enclosure: CV

Direct approach to a potential employer (senior R&D engineer)

From: Samantha Robinson [srobinson@email.com]
To: Recipient's e-mail address
Cc:
Subject: R&D-to-market problems?

Dear Recipient's Name,

If your R&D-to-market time needs a sense of urgency, creativity and a seasoned coordinator of people and priorities, we should talk. As a senior R&D Engineer this is what I do, and have done successfully with 73 new products:

- STRATEGIC PLANNING: Etched long- and short-term technological plans that kept a £2bn manufacturer ahead of its competition since 20–

- COORDINATED RESOURCES: 20+ years in planning, reviewing and benchmarking technical performance, meeting budgetary goals, and coordinating interlaboratory and interdepartmental efforts

- ENRICHED KNOWLEDGE: New-product training for sales, marketing, and technical staffs worldwide

- MOVED THE MARKET TO OUR PRODUCT: Expert at using technology to create markets

- IMPECCABLE RECORD: Achieved 70 to 80 per cent first-time success rate in field testing for all products developed; hold x no. UK patents; consulted worldwide by engineers and scientists; published; presenter at technical conferences since post-doctoral fellowship

Reviewing my credentials and past results, you will note they occurred in the XYZ field. However, I am confident the core *technical, engineering and organizational expertise would readily adapt* to ABC Ltd because in R&D-to-market, while the products may be different, the concerns remain constant.

If you need a *driven problem solver who can get your staff focused, motivated and productive*, I am readily available to discuss how I can channel my more than two decades of success to your POSITION at ABC LTD. Please see my attached CV. I look forward to talking.

Yours sincerely,

Samantha Robinson
0123456 7890
Attachment: CV

Direct approach to a potential employer (multilingual sales manager)

Robert Rodriguez

1 Any Street ~ Anytown AA1 1AA
Mobile: 1098765 4321 ~ Pager: 123456 7890 ~ E-mail: robrodriguez@hotmail.com

Fluent in Spanish… time management skills… eight years' front-line experience… service-orientated positions… trainer… presentation expertise…

(Date)

Emily _____
(Title)
ABC Ltd
1 Industry Plaza
Anytown AA1 1AA

Dear Ms _____,

If you know your *customers and operations deserve attention to detail*, as well as a high-energy individual who is *fluent in Spanish and makes people a number 1 priority*, I am one individual you need to interview for a ZYX position at ABC Ltd.

Reviewing my credentials, you will note that I have taught in a secondary school for the past eight years. This exposure to *daily planning, keeping people motivated and moving* ahead can be an immediate asset at ABC, and here are some areas that align with your needs:

- SUCCESS IN DIRECT COMMUNICATION: Whether with students, decision-makers or the general public, my presentation skills kept people interested, involved and properly served…

- MULTILINGUAL ABILITIES: Fluent in Spanish, Japanese and Russian – despite having a Spanish-only background, mastered the dialects of Russian and Japanese and was teaching classes…

- ALWAYS LOOKING FOR IMPROVEMENTS: Successfully integrated technology with additional conversational strategies… working for a distributor as an undergraduate, took initiative to revamp routing – increased productivity and service… increased a student's competency from 31 per cent to 100 per cent while a student…

- FOCUS ON SERVICE: Made individual needs a priority as a teacher – adept at varying approach to suit individual personalities and priorities…

- MOTIVATED: Worked up to 30 hours weekly while pursuing degree… proven abilities to juggle diverse assignments opened door for additional assignments and leadership roles…

Page 1 of 2

Robert Rodriguez
Page 2 of 2

I want to channel my communication, presentation, customer service, training and organizational skills, and the ZYX opportunity at ABC Ltd matches my goal for a transferable opportunity. *You would benefit from someone with a proven track record in front-line positions, and your customers and operations will have a team player who knows how to set goals, meet goals and keep customers' needs at the forefront.*

I will take the liberty of contacting you on _____ at _____ to confirm your receipt of my information and briefly discuss how my energy and talents could be your asset. I would also like to arrange a meeting at that time. Should you need to reach me sooner, I can be contacted at 12345 678910 or robrodriguez@hotmail.com.

Yours sincerely,

Robert Rodriguez

Robert Rodriguez

Enclosure: CV

Direct approach to a potential employer (management)

LORI PAULEY

1 Any Street • Anytown AA1 1AA • 12345 678910

(Date)
Phillip _____
(Title)
ABC Ltd
1 Industry Plaza
Anytown AA1 1AA

Dear Mr _____,

People will only give you what you're willing to accept. That's why my staff employed the Golden Rule every day, treating customers the way they themselves would like to be treated.

If you need someone with a technical background who has hired and kept top talent challenged and on their toes delivering exemplary service, then consider that in 20+ years:

- I turned my knowledge of physics and business into profits and operational success – for my staff, my employers, and myself.

- I took on the lead engineering position in my second year with an industry giant, skipping over the traditional 12-year career path – I simply outworked everyone and never said I couldn't do something or get it done on time or within budget.

- I earned full latitude in decision making after proving my team's understanding of a new target market's needs – I introduced more products than my successors, improved processes, and cut manufacturing and warranty costs by roughly £1m the first year.

- Operations I had an impact on experienced extremely low employee turnover – and employees met or exceeded customer expectations 100 per cent of the time.

I've made sure my staff are so service-oriented that the customer doesn't have to ask for warranty repairs or 'the next step' – they have the answers or have already performed the warranty work.

And when my name is on a project, it is always on schedule, within budget – and is a winner:

- When a relationship with a speciality manufacturer ended, I spearheaded development of an intake manifold line, analysed and negotiated manufacturing costs, and selected vendors – and launched an 18-unit product line in 18 months that led the industry.

- The first race manifold we developed took the first five finishes in the 19– motorsport race without prior testing by participating teams.

Page 1 of 2

Lori Pauley
Page 2 of 2

If you seek someone with the work ethic of a business partner, then I am your top choice for the
_____ opportunity with ABC Ltd. I fully understand the nuts-and-bolts of customer
service, and can certainly combine my financial know-how with proven success in the field at
ABC.

Right now I'm ready to step down from entrepreneurial management, simplify my role, and do
'one or three things' well for an organization that values integrity, hard work and creativity.

If I sound like the person you need at ABC, then contact me right away to discuss the
_____ opportunity. I can be reached on 12345 678910 after 6 pm Monday to
Friday, or at my place of business on 10987 654321 during regular business hours. I will take the
liberty of contacting you on Monday at 10 am to briefly screen my qualifications and see if we
can arrange an interview.

Yours sincerely,

Lori Pauley

Lori Pauley

Enclosure: CV

Direct approach to a potential employer (HR generalist)

Elliott Davidson
1 Any Street
Anytown AA1 1AA
12345 678910 • davidsonhrpro@msn.com

HR GENERALIST
9 years advising senior decision-makers on employee matters…
5 years in pension administration for £1bn company and 5 affiliates…
15 years delivering HR presentations…
Open enrolment/pension processing for professional employees…
13 years' grievance/disciplinary meeting involvement…
10+ years' training/development, entry through professional levels…
Worked through mergers and reorganizations…
Created award-winning concept for enrolment booklet…
Earned highest ratings throughout career…

(Date)

Phillip _____
(Title)
ABC Ltd
1 Industry Plaza
Anytown AA1 1AA

Dear Mr _____,

If your organization seeks someone to advance your human resource programmes, consider my proven track record. I am ready for a challenge with ABC Ltd, as your recent growth needs someone used to working with new subsidiaries and maintaining the bottom line. I am absolutely ready to step in as your Human Resource Director at ABC Ltd, as my commitment extends to all areas you seek to address.

I bring you and your employees objectivity, knowledge of policy/procedure implementation and interpretation, and hands-on work in an ever-emerging climate. Here are some highlighted abilities that can be put to work immediately at ABC Ltd:

MET THE CHALLENGE: With little notification, stepped in and was an asset in a HR Directorship capacity; administered £20m in pension benefits; initiated multi-tier health plan to better suit regional product needs

Page 1 of 2

ELLIOTT DAVIDSON
Page 2 of 2

BENEFITS: Five years working with open enrolment for all levels of employees – restructured pensions during three internal reorganizations

REMAINED FLEXIBLE: Adapted to the needs of entrepreneurial organizations while continuing a career with major utility company

LEADERSHIP: Entrusted to step in for superiors due to track record in HR; number 1 person consulted by senior managers of a £1bn parent company and its five affiliates regarding HR or pensions; negotiated with union leadership, discussed and resolved grievances and complaints

COMMUNITY INVOLVEMENT: Accepted leadership role in major charity organization, keynote speaker for regional fundraising appearances

TRAINING/DEVELOPMENT: Delivered HR and pensions presentations since 1995, safety training, two years

OVER/ABOVE: Travelled over three-year period to help a newly formed company whose explosive growth took it to 2,000 employees in three years (coordinated staffing and pension enrolment while maintaining existing workload); singled out for HR support for special finance division structure, took on policy making/interpretation and HR

If you need someone seasoned in policy making who can interface with decision-makers and keep you 100 per cent compliant with regulations, I am one individual awaiting your call for an interview.

I will call on Monday at 10 am to see if you agree that my background could be an immediate asset, and to arrange a meeting. I can forward a CV for your review immediately. Should you need to reach me sooner, I am on 12345 678910.

Yours sincerely,

Elliott Davidson

Elliott Davidson

~ Pensions ~ Multi-tier Coverage ~ Labour Relations ~ Grievances ~ Arbitration ~
Job Bidding ~ CPP, CRS, PDS ~ Redundancy Compensation ~ Sexual Harassment ~
Safety Training ~ Background Investigations ~

Direct approach to a potential employer (operations manager)

A redundant environmental operations manager is trying to get back into a tight job market.

Diane Baldwin
1 Any Street ■ Anytown AA1 1AA
12345 678910 ■ operationsmanager@alphone.net

(Date)

ABD Ltd
1 Industry Plaza
Anytown AA1 1AA
Attention Ms Emily_____

Dear Ms_____,

Do you need an experienced, versatile individual who can improve bottom-line profits? I can bring innovative ideas to the position of Operations Manager – ideas that can benefit a service-driven, quality-orientated company like yours. No one has money to burn in a tough economy, which is why adding a ready skilled manager to your staff can reduce time and money.

The match between your needs and my talents is ideal. Why? Because my strengths lie in understanding the labour and manufacturing operations that design, build, install and manage equipment for environmental and production improvements. I am a leader both by example and through effective management of individuals and teams. In short, I have the drive and vision to make a positive difference in any organization.

Dozens of proposed projects have been successfully implemented due to my established reputation for the quality of work completed. The work performed under my direction has come in at, or below, budget and we meet project deadlines.

The enclosed CV summarizes my qualifications and achievements. I would be glad to discuss any of this information with you as an opportunity for employment. Because 'proven skills' are best explained in person, I look forward to our conversation and will call early next week to arrange a meeting. Thank you for taking the time to review my CV and for your consideration.

Yours sincerely,

Diane Baldwin

Diane Baldwin

Enclosure: CV

Direct approach to a potential employer (pharmaceutical sales)

From: Rebecca Marks [rmarks@email.com]
To: Recipient's e-mail address
Cc:
Subject: Entry-level Pharmaceutical Sales

Dear Recipient's Name,

ABC Laboratories is one of the fastest-growing companies in the United Kingdom and I am eager to make a contribution to your professional team as a Pharmaceutical Sales Representative.

As a recent graduate with a BA in marketing, my professional experience is limited. However, I believe that you will find that I exhibit intelligence, common sense, initiative, maturity and stability. The jobs I have held have all required a good attitude and keen interpersonal skills. These jobs, along with my education, life experience and extensive travels, have given me a totally different paradigm compared to other applicants.

Analysing an audience is of utmost importance as a sales representative. As the daughter of a physician, I had extensive exposure to the medical environment. I strongly believe this gives me insight into the way physicians think – that patients' needs come first. Therefore, effective presentations of products must be made in a timely, succinct, and caring manner for successful sales in this industry. My desire is to stay close to the medical field, and working in a pharmaceutical company is exactly where I aspire to be.

After reviewing the attached CV, please contact me on 12345 678910 to arrange an interview. I look forward to discussing how my qualifications can meet your personnel needs and contribute to your company's important mission.

Yours sincerely,

Rebecca Marks
12345 678910
Attachment: CV

Direct approach to a potential employer (information technology programme manager)

DARRYL C WARREN

1 Any Street
Anytown AA1 1AA

12345 678910
ITpro@yahoo.com

(Date)

Mr Philip _____
CEO
ABC
1 Industry Plaza
Anytown AA1 1AA

Dear Mr _____,

May I ask your advice and assistance?

As a result of XYZ's merger with DEF Bank, I am confidentially exploring my opportunities. Although I am confident that I will be offered a role in the new organization, I am currently assessing where I can make the optimal contribution.

I am an Information Technology Programme Manager. In this role, I have led the development of key financial systems and strategic business plans, co-managed the seamless migration of two divisions to another region and founded the GHI Networking Group – delivering noteworthy cost savings and productivity gains. For the past 11 years, I've had dream jobs with leading firms like XYZ and JKL Consulting. I have been entrusted with the direction of large-scale global projects. Many times I learned 'on my feet' – to implement new systems, design testing methods, manage resources, repair damaged vendor relations for mutual gain, and to meet a wide array of challenges. My career has accelerated based on the results, as you'll note from the accomplishments in my enclosed CV.

I'm considering transferring my skills and experience to an organization where I can continue to be a team player and visionary leader for state-of-the-art technology programmes, and where I'll also continue to learn new functional and technical areas. My expertise and interests are in the financial service industry.

I would greatly appreciate a few minutes of your time to discuss my options and glean any suggestions you can offer. I'll phone you in a few days to see if we can arrange a brief meeting.

Thanks very much.

Yours sincerely,

Darryl Warren

Darryl Warren

Enclosure: CV

Direct approach to a potential employer (director of operations)

A retiree in his late fifties, Barry is still interested in full-time employment and wants to communicate this to his contacts without giving the impression that he is 'old' and 'set in his ways'. The tone of the letter is intended to be energetic and full of youthful enthusiasm.

Barry D Hargrove

1 Any Street • Anytown AA1 1AA • 12345 678910 • operationsvp@yahoo.com

(Date)

Philip _____, (Title)
ABC Equipment
1 Industry Plaza
Anytown AA1 1AA

Dear Mr _____,

Problem – Action – Results. It is a simple formula, and one that I have implemented successfully throughout my long career in manufacturing. A former business associate passed your name on to me after commenting that my business philosophy and style reminded him of a CEO he had heard speak at a conference in Luton. That CEO was you.

It has been several years since I took my first job as a machinist back in Birmingham, but I have never lost my enthusiasm for finding faster and better ways to accomplish goals while cutting costs. I have worked my way up through the ranks from Foreman, to Supervisor, to Manufacturing Engineer, to Operations Manager, and finally Director of Operations. Taking a shot at every new idea that came my way, I may have missed a few, but overall my success rate has been good:

- led a £340m manufacturing firm to earning ISO9002 certification on first attempt;
- revitalized operations at a plant site in Romania by implementing a comprehensive employee training programme;
- increased profits by 200 per cent by identifying and rectifying problems with production and delivery at a Romanian manufacturing facility.

I believe strongly in teams and am comfortable working with R&D, engineering and marketing professionals. My colleagues have expressed appreciation for my direct and honest approach to people and problems.

Between jobs now, I am planning a fishing excursion in Ireland. I will be arriving in London on 20th March and would like to get together with you to explore potential opportunities with ABC Equipment. It would be great to meet over lunch. I will give you a call the morning of the 22nd to see if that can be arranged.

I'm sending you my CV to lay a foundation for our meeting. I look forward to meeting you and exchanging ideas.

Yours sincerely,

Barry Hargrove

Enclosure: CV

Direct approach to a potential employer (consultant)

A retired executive wants to approach companies directly and offer her unique expertise on a contract or consulting basis.

From: Elizabeth Jameson [ejameson@email.com]
To: Recipient's e-mail address
Cc:
Subject: IT performance, disaster recovery, information security

Dear Recipient's Name,

- **Is your organization fully prepared to safeguard its technology services, information and facilities in the event of a disaster?**
- **Are you taking full advantage of high-value and cost-effective vendor agreements?**
- **Do you benefit from high team performance and low turnover?**

If you have answered 'No' to any of the above questions, then allow me to introduce myself and the expertise I can offer your organization.

My expertise is delivering results. I design, implement and optimize comprehensive enterprise-class disaster recovery and information security procedures.

- **Expert in Disaster Recovery, Information Security and Business Continuity** – expertise includes planning, protection and off-site recovery of technology services, databases and facilities
- **Superior contract procurement, negotiation and vendor management capabilities** – proven record for negotiating agreements that improve service quality and save millions in vendor costs
- **Strong, decisive and motivating leader** – reputation for building and leading high-performance teams to breakthrough achievement

These abilities have saved millions in vendor negotiations and third-party service agreements, and led a variety of cross-functional teams to consistently achieve and exceed organizational mandates.

If this interests you, I invite you to review the attached CV. I am available for full-time, part-time, contract and consulting assignments.

I thank you for your consideration and I look forward to speaking to you soon.

Yours sincerely,

Elizabeth Jameson
0123456 7890
Attachment: CV

Direct approach to a potential employer (project manager)

MICHAEL J SALINGER

1 Any Street • Anytown AA1 1AA • 12345 678910

(Date)

Dear Recipient's Name,

Because of current market conditions and high unemployment, I am sure you have many applicants and few **Project or Training Manager** positions to fill. With this letter and CV, please allow me to add to the list; but, may I also give a few reasons why you might want to call me ahead of other qualified candidates should an appropriate position become available?

You will note that my educational and professional **background is broad** and includes experience in post-secondary organizations, community colleges, business and the army. Because of this range of experience, I am able to bring **insight and the ability to relate well to individuals at all levels and from diverse backgrounds**.

Working within for-profit organizations has enabled me to develop an **eye for the bottom line**. Whether it be budgetary or profit-enhancing, I am continually evaluating systems and methods to make them more efficient and productive.

Incredible as it may sound, I appreciate and welcome change. I am **known for my abilities as a change agent**. However, while I may embrace change – technologically or otherwise – I recognize that many do not. Therefore, from a management standpoint, I look for ways to make transitions more tolerable for the people in my charge.

While my CV is comprehensive, it does not fully demonstrate the manner in which I have achieved success. My character, personality and the ability to lead a project or team effectively could be evidenced in a personal meeting. Therefore, I would welcome an interview to discuss your needs and my qualifications further. Thank you for your time and consideration.

Yours sincerely,

Michael Salinger

Michael Salinger

Enclosure: CV

Direct approach to a potential employer
(senior buyer/purchasing agent/purchasing manager)

From: Kalista Jabert [purchasingpro@earthlink.net]
To: Recipient's e-mail address
Cc:
Subject: Smart Purchasing Choice

Dear Recipient's Name,

Do you cringe at the high costs your company incurs for goods and services?

Do you need someone who will maximize vendor resources, working hard to secure lower-cost, longer-term contracts?

Do you need someone on board who will immediately slash supply costs and streamline purchasing operations?

With more than 20 years in purchasing, retail sales management, store expansions and new product research and market launch, I believe I may offer just what you're missing.

In my career with Major Company, a premier auto parts and accessories distributor, I have:

- directed procurement of over £200m of goods and services, accounting for 60 per cent of MC's total purchasing budget;
- launched three private label programmes, garnering £500K in additional profits during the first year of distribution;
- recouped £300K in stolen merchandise and prosecuted the employees responsible;
- generated £3m in savings by cultivating partnerships and negotiating long-term contracts with key suppliers.

If you're tired of seeing your company's profits slip through your fingers, please review my attached CV and call me today to arrange a meeting. I can't wait to discuss how I can benefit your purchasing operation right away.

Yours sincerely,

Kalista Jabert
12345 678910
Attachment: CV

Direct approach to a potential employer (new product marketing)

From: Elizabeth Stettin [marketingexpert@aol.com]
To: Recipient's e-mail address
Cc:
Subject: Real Marketing Savvy

Dear Recipient's Name,

If you are looking for a successful executive to take charge of new product marketing, you will be interested in talking to me.

Ten years' experience in every aspect of marketing and sales in different industries gives me the confidence to be open to opportunities in almost any field. My search is focused on companies that innovate, because I am particularly effective at new product marketing. I have successfully managed new product-marketing research, launch planning, advertising, product training and sales support, as well as direct sales. In my current position with XYZ Company, I created several products and marketing approaches on which other operating divisions in the company based their programmes.

My business education includes a Marketing MBA from _____ University's School of Management, and provides me with a variety of useful analytical tools in managing problems and maximizing opportunities. My superior sales track record guarantees that I bring the reality of the marketplace to each business situation; I know what sells and why.

Currently, my total salary package is in the low seventies. I am looking for a company that rewards performance consistently.

Since I am presently weighing up several interesting opportunities, please contact me immediately if you are conducting any searches that might be a good fit. Relocation is no problem.

Thank you in advance for your consideration.

Yours sincerely,

Elizabeth Stettin
12345 678910
Attachment: CV

Direct approach to a potential employer (career change – marketing to finance)

From: Your Name [Your e-mail address]
To: Recipient's e-mail address
Cc:
Subject: Finance: Accounting Manager/Director, Controller/Treasurer

Dear Recipient's Name,

I have ten years' successful experience within financial services marketing, and will receive my CPA within two months. With this unique combination of skills and awareness, I now hope to move into a more distinct financial management position such as accounting Manager, Controller, or Treasurer.

As an Account Manager in financial services, I know many different industries, and my marketing knowledge would be of unusual benefit to any company seeking someone with these titles.

My understanding of the revenue generating function and the revenue protection and leveraging function, especially of financial services companies, gives me a very special frame of reference on my chosen path. As an executive recruiter, I am sure you can appreciate this.

I have attached my CV, which will flesh out my unusual and desirable background; I would appreciate your input. I am available for interviews, and can be reached at 01345 67890. Please consider me available as a resource for your other searches within my profession.

Yours sincerely,

Your Name
01345 67890
Attachment: CV

Direct approach to a potential employer (consultative sales and account management)

From: Your Name [Your e-mail address]
To: Recipient's e-mail address
Cc:
Subject: Consultative sales and account management

Dear Recipient's Name,

If you need a top-performing Sales Manager with expertise in new business development, consultative sales, account management, and product/service development, I offer a proven track record of combining big picture strategic planning with day-to-day tactics that have consistently delivered improvements in market share and bottom-line profits. For example:

- Most recently, as Regional Sales Manager for _____ , I brought in a multi-year contract with £4 million in annual revenues.
- For the same employer, I launched a programme for a client with 2,100 stores that deliver approximately £1.55 million in sales.
- As Sales Manager for _____ , I innovated strategic marketing/co-op partnerships that delivered win/win outcomes with companies such as _____ , _____ , and _____ .

My greatest strengths include my ability to forge strong client relationships, build and motivate sales teams, and innovate new products and processes that drive substantial revenue contributions.

I am currently seeking a new professional challenge with a company in which I can make a strong and sustained contribution.

While my attached CV provides an overview of my past performance, I look forward to a personal meeting at which we can discuss your needs and my qualifications in detail. Thank you for your consideration.

Yours sincerely,

Your Name
0123456 7890
Attachment: CV

Direct approach to a potential employer (customer service)

From: Your Name [Your e-mail address]
To: Recipient's e-mail address
Cc:
Subject: Customer Service Specialist, organized, calm, analytical, solution-orientated

Dear Recipient's Name,

Are you looking for a Senior Customer Service Specialist who is:

- A team player able to achieve results through coordination with employees in all functional areas?
- An effective communicator with excellent writing, training, and telephone skills?
- Able to learn quickly, analyse complex information, and find solutions to problems?
- Organized, thorough, and precise?

If so, you will be interested in my qualifications. I have a BA in Business Administration and 7 years' experience in the insurance/financial industries, serving as Customer Relations Advisor and Calculations Processor.

I consistently receive the highest rating in my unit despite the fact that the difficult cases frequently find their way to my desk. I also contribute to my team by putting in extra time to clear backlogs and analysing existing procedures to devise more efficient methods of operation.

My CV is attached for your review. If you think that I can make a positive contribution to _____ , I look forward to meeting you to discuss my qualifications in detail. Thank you for your time and consideration.

Yours sincerely,

Your Name
0123456 7890
Attachment: CV

Direct approach to a potential employer (direction shift within sales)

From: Your Name [Your e-mail address]
To: Recipient's e-mail address
Cc:
Subject: B-to-B sales professional

Dear Recipient's Name,

Having spent five years as an executive recruiter, I realize how many CVs you receive on a daily basis. I also remember how valuable a few always turned out to be.

My background, skills, and talents are in all aspects of sales and sales management. As job search is the only field of sales where the products talk back, I am confident that my skills will readily translate into less complex sales environments. My research indicates that your expertise is in this broad Sales/Marketing area.

I have attached my CV, which highlights my skills and supports my objectives. I would appreciate the opportunity to meet and exchange ideas. I will call you over the next few days to make an appointment. If you prefer, you may reach me by e-mail or in the evening at 01234 567890.

Thank you; I look forward to speaking further with you.

Yours sincerely,

Your Name
01234 567890
Attachment: CV

Direct approach to a potential employer (EMEA account management)

From: Your Name [Your e-mail address]
To: Recipient's e-mail address
Cc:
Subject: EMEA Account Management

Dear Recipient's Name,

It has been said, *'in today's world there are two kinds of companies – the quick and the dead.'*
I propose the same is true of managers. I am a dynamic sales management professional with
extraordinary team-building and interpersonal skills, and thrive in a global market.

I've held direct responsibility for commercial dealings with the UK, Ireland, and Germany; bilingual,
my translation skills are strong in both languages. I also have conversational knowledge of French.
I have a remarkable knack for capturing key client relations with diverse cultures and people. I would
like to bring my business knowledge and management/marketing skills to your company.

My experience spans Property Development, International Affairs, and Procurement, a frame of
reference relevant to any company with global aspirations. I never run from a difficult situation.
If you want a successful outcome, you can count on it – accurately, punctually, and right the first
time.

Dedicated to doing whatever it takes to achieve outstanding results, I will lead your team to meet
tight deadlines. In short, I will not let you down. Outstanding references will verify these claims.

Please see my attached CV. I look forward to meeting you to discuss your needs and the immediate
impact I can make.

Yours sincerely,

Your Name
0123456 7890
Attachment: CV

Direct approach to a potential employer (EMEA executive sales leader)

From: Your Name [Your e-mail address]
To: Recipient's e-mail address
Cc:
Subject: EMEA Marketing challenges conquered

Dear Recipient's Name,

As a performance-focused Executive Sales Leader with two decades of experience working within the EMEA, APAC, and US markets, I have a history of accelerating growth through the introduction of best management, channel sales development, and operating practices that achieve world-class status and business sustainability.

One of my greatest strengths lies in my ability to define and implement critical strategies to heighten revenue growth, expand market share, and substantially improve overall customer service. For example, with my position at (Company) I have provided all strategic annual planning for a £250 million business. During this time I also led a 20 per cent growth in new software licensing business.

My experience includes overseeing a P&L of more than £50 million, while driving performance of large teams located around the globe. I believe my skills in direct, channel, inside, and online sales of SaaS, cloud, telecommunications, and software sales could be a great fit for your organization.

Capable of devising smart solutions to complex business issues, I also bring honed skills in collaborative leadership, communication, and flexibility. A few examples of my record of accomplishments include:

- Led turnaround of key products and services line of business from a £3 million annual loss to £12 million profit within two years.
- Drove 31 per cent growth in software and subscription revenue, 78 per cent sales margin, and 15 per cent increase in business partner productivity within one year.
- Grew SaaS services revenue more than 110 per cent in 18 months by driving international expansion of Managed Service Partner network and Eco-System.
- Aligned organization for rapid expansion through sourcing and closing deals with FT Global 500 partners in the UK market, focusing on verticals in Finance, High Tech, and Health Care.

My CV is attached and I look forward to hearing from you in the near future to arrange an interview whereby I may learn more about your company's plans and goals and how I can contribute to its continued success.

Yours sincerely,

Your Name
0123456 7890
Attachment: CV

Direct approach to a potential employer (entry-level chemical engineer)

From: Your Name [Your e-mail address]
To: Recipient's e-mail address
Cc:
Subject: Entry-Level Chemical Engineer

Dear Recipient's Name,

Following my recent graduation from _____ University with a **Bachelor of Science Degree in Chemical Engineering**, I am currently seeking an entry-level position in the Energy Industry. I offer more than two years of hands-on experience, a strong work ethic, and commitment to personal and company success.

Representative of my qualifications and accomplishments:

- Graduated with a first-class honours degree.
- Gained valuable hands-on laboratory experience as a Lab Assistant for two years in the *ABC Engineering Lab*, working on nanoparticle suspension projects.
- Completed a summer internship with _____ *Nutrition*, where I experienced and managed real-world corporate challenges and honed team-based communication skills.

I work hard, contribute, collaborate, and strive to deliver strong and sustained contributions to organizational goals. I learn quickly, thrive on challenges, and am flexible in adapting to new environments. I am always willing to go the extra mile, no matter what the task.

While my CV provides an overview of my past performance, I look forward to a personal meeting at which we can discuss my desire to start at the bottom and earn the right to become a respected member of your team. Thank you for your consideration.

Yours sincerely,

Your Name
0123456 7890
Attachment: CV

Direct approach to a potential employer (finance management)

From: Your Name [Your e-mail address]
To: Recipient's e-mail address
Cc:
Subject: Finance Management with CPA

Dear Recipient's Name,

As a Certified Public Accountant with solid experience as a **Chief Financial Officer** and a **Director of Finance**, I understand that success depends on the bottom line, with special attention to financial and managerial teamwork. I believe that my background and accomplishments have proven to be a productive combination.

Throughout my career, I have been assigned increasing responsibilities and significantly contributed to corporate growth in Architectural, Engineering, and Construction sectors. Here are some accomplishments:

- Increased shareholder distribution from zero in ____ to £1.3 million and £1.5 million in ____ and ____ , respectively, in spite of a 20 per cent revenue shrinkage over the same time period.
- Improved cash flow more than £3 million in 6 months.
- Grew profit margin from 3 per cent to 10 per cent for 3 consecutive years, *the best in company history*.
- Reduced overhead from 170 per cent to 120 per cent in direct labour.
- Trimmed DOS 21 per cent from 85 to 67 days.

Thank you for your consideration. Please see my attached CV. I look forward to speaking with you to discuss how I might make a positive contribution to your operation.

Yours sincerely,

Your Name
0123456 7890
Attachment: CV

Direct approach to a potential employer (mutual funds advisor)

From: Your Name [Your e-mail address]
To: Recipient's e-mail address
Cc:
Subject: Financial advisor: mutual fund research, high net worth, asset management, mutual fund analytics

Dear Recipient's Name,

I am an investment professional with unique experience as both a financial advisor and someone who has sold to financial advisors. I also have considerable complementary experience in mutual fund research and work with high-net-worth investors.

With 16+ years' experience in asset management, mutual fund analytics, sales, marketing, research, client relationship management, financial advising, and more, my experience gives me unusual insight into the nuances of investment strategy and client relationship management – assets **consistently recognized** by my employers.

At _____ , as a Senior Sales Consultant, I have developed a solid reputation for raising the bar and establishing greater visibility and credibility for our team's professional role. I am interested in talking to you about opportunities at _____ , involving investment analysis, product management, mutual fund investment strategy analysis, and product and platform analytics and research.

I have attached my CV to furnish you with specifics regarding my background, skills, and experience, and I am confident that you will find sufficient merit in my qualifications to warrant further investigation.

Thank you for your courtesy in reviewing my qualifications. I look forward to the opportunity to discuss my ability to make a meaningful contribution toward your goals.

Yours sincerely,

Your Name
0123456 7890
Attachment: CV

Direct approach to a potential employer (relocation for application developer)

From: Your Name [Your e-mail address]
To: Recipient's e-mail address
Co:
Subject: Application Developer

Dear Recipient's Name,

As an Application Developer I am very interested in joining your software development team. You have long been on my radar as a major innovator. You have a reputation for quality products, customer support, and being a great employer, and I want to work in an environment in which application development is critical.

My current position is Application Developer for _____ . The job has provided me with three years' hands-on experience in Visual Basic and other languages. However, I am eager to jump into actual software writing, as well as returning to the _____ area.

I have a BSc in Computer Science and am getting close to completing my Master's Degree.

My CV is attached for your review. I'll be back in _____ in three weeks, so I am going to call you to arrange a meeting for when I visit. In the meantime, please feel free to e-mail or call for further information. Thank you for your consideration. I look forward to meeting you in the near future.

Yours sincerely,

Your Name
0123456 7890
Attachment: CV

Direct approach to a potential employer (research–reference librarian)

From: Your Name [Your e-mail address]
To: Recipient's e-mail address
Cc:
Subject: Research/Reference Librarian

Dear Recipient's Name,

Are you looking for an **Entry-Level Research or Reference Librarian or Cataloguer**?
My experience with Internet resources and navigational tools, combined with my experience with library databases, affords you the opportunity to hire an entry-level library professional with proven librarianship success.

With my recent MSc in Information Management from _____ , as well as internship experience in the reference department of academic and government libraries, perhaps I can be of service.

My CV is attached for your review; in it you will find information on my education, training, and work experience. I would like to draw your attention to credentials that are out of the norm:

- Fluent Polish, Russian, Slovak, German, Latin
- Taught English and Civics, pass rate of 100 per cent over 8-year period: 2000 foreign students
- Voyager Module, AACR2r, LC classification scheme, MARC format, and OCLC, as well as Lexis-Nexis, Dow Jones, Dialog Web, and Classic

Providing high-level customer service and efficiency is my goal in library services. Can we meet soon to discuss your needs? I will call your office next week to arrange a mutually convenient appointment. Thank you for your time and consideration.

Yours sincerely,

Your Name
0123456 7890
Attachment: CV

Direct approach to a potential employer (senior EMEA marketing)

From: Your Name [Your e-mail address]
To: Recipient's e-mail address
Cc:
Subject: Senior EMEA Marketing

Dear Recipient's Name,

I am a Senior EMEA Marketing professional with stellar Asian sector successes who has leaped over cultural barriers to forge some of the most profitable technical opportunities in the telecommunications and construction fields.

I received three promotions in the last four years due to my success in managing contacts, motivating staff, and implementing marketing campaigns that tripled ROI. My work in strategic partnering, developing alliances, creating new opportunities, and exceeding multinational clients' expectations has helped my employers more than double their sales. Some repeatable highlights:

- Market data and voice communication services to multinational corporations and Internet service providers in Japan, Southeast Asia, Canada, and Western Europe.
- Delivered 28 global accounts representing up to a 250 per cent sales increase.
- Created the first transcontinental ATM circuit.
- Added £1.5 million in sales, with an add-on service option.
- Partnered parent company with Japan-based joint venture interests that enabled the first European-built airport in Japan. Landed two additional opportunities for a total of £10 million in business in one year.

Reviewing my attached CV, you will note Doctoral, Master's, and Bachelor's degrees – quantifiable results and extensive technical training that serve only to enhance my drive and enthusiasm. I will gladly set aside time to meet you and discuss how my knowledge of technology, client relations, and strategic partnering can become your biggest asset.

Yours sincerely,

Your Name
0123456 7890
Attachment: CV

Direct approach to a potential employer (senior PR professional)

From: Your Name [Your e-mail address]
To: Recipient's e-mail address
Cc:
Subject: Olympic performance in PR

Dear Recipient's Name,

Saw you quoted on the _____ blog last week, and your comments made me smile: 'everyone sees the gleaming results, no one sees the blood, sweat, and tears that lead to them.' I believe I might have something of interest to say.

An Olympic gold-medal winner and 12-year high-tech public relations professional, I am passionate about achieving results for my clients and team. My track record for delivering successful strategic PR, executive communications, and leadership positioning is demonstrated by ten years of client loyalty. I am a dynamic professional with extraordinary team-building and interpersonal skills, and I thrive in the competitive environment that is PR.

My complementary experience as a television commentator, coupled with 20 years as a professional public speaker, give me real validity when advising, coaching, and media-training clients and executives.

In my attached CV you will find proof points for my PR acumen including:

- Demonstrated track record of strategic communications and influential public relations
- Accomplished media relations/story placement, from ABC News to XYZNet
- Team, account, budget, client, and executive management
- Client loyalty and satisfaction
- Considerable network of high-tech industry players
- New business success
- Self-motivated team player

Thank you in advance for reviewing my CV. Please contact me at your earliest convenience to arrange an interview.

Yours sincerely,

Your Name
0123456 7890
Attachment: CV

Direct approach to a potential employer (warehouse logistics)

From: Your Name [Your e-mail address]
To: Recipient's e-mail address
Co:
Subject: Warehouse Manager, assembly/expediting/scheduling/shipping/receiving/
          order fulfilment/customer service

Dear Recipient's Name,

If you are in need of a Warehouse Manager/Inventory Control Specialist/Production Manager or Assembly Order Fulfilment Supervisor, please consider my track record: 15 years' experience in assembly, expediting and scheduling, shipping and receiving, order fulfilment, customer service, sales, supervision, and training.

I have a verifiable track record of meeting deadlines in demanding situations:

- Efficiently scheduled assembly, material handlers, and warehouse personnel, and closely monitored interplant transfers of raw materials from 20 warehouses. Assembly production and distribution procedures yielded high levels of productivity: 90 per cent on-time delivery, including emergency orders, of up to £1 million in SKUs per week.
- As final assembly and inspection member of 4-person team, met heavy production schedule (35 to 60 complex, fabricated units per day) with 6 per cent or less error rate.
- Working as part of a team, created, tested, packaged, and directed to shipping custom ship sets of complex hose assemblies, meeting deadlines 99-plus per cent of the time.

It is hard-working and cooperative people who deliver results. My focus on teamwork and productivity has always proven successful in past assignments. I am competent, enthusiastic, with a strong work ethic, dedicated, and dependable – I get the job done right.

May we meet soon to discuss your needs? Please review my attached CV. Thank you for your consideration.

Yours sincerely,

Your Name
0123456 7890
Attachment: CV

Direct approach to a recruitment professional (health care)

Adam has developed strong relationships with clinics, hospitals and physicians throughout his career. He wants to use this experience to gain a position with a clinic, capitalizing on his expertise in preventive health and chronic illness management programmes.

From: Adam G Stevens [agstevens@email.com]
To: Recipient's e-mail address
Cc:
Subject: Health Management Professional

Dear Recipient's Name,

With a 20-plus-year track record in the pharmaceutical industry, I believe that I have unique talents that could benefit a clinic or health care organization. Some of the key capabilities that I can bring to a new opportunity include:

- *Design and implementation of health management programmes. Firsthand experience developing programmes for asthma management, and directing programmes that have delivered substantial savings to client companies.*

- *Managing the development and implementation of web-based services that are new revenue centres for my company and value-added services to its physician customer base.*

- *Exceptional account relations skills. I currently call on and maintain business relationships with key client contacts at the highest levels.*

- *A broader understanding of health care gained through extensive interaction with health care professionals at all levels.*

- *Certification from the University of London in Quality Management and from the National Heart, Lung & Blood Institute.*

I am confident that my knowledge and expertise would allow me to deliver successful results for one of your clients in the health care service. I would enjoy speaking to you in person to explore potential opportunities. Please review my attached CV. You can call or e-mail me to arrange a convenient time for us to meet. As my employer is unaware of my job search, I trust that you will hold this correspondence in strict confidence and consult with me before releasing my materials to a prospective employer.

Thank you for your time and consideration. I look forward to talking to you soon.

Yours sincerely,

Adam G Stevens
0123456 7890
Attachment: CV

Direct approach to a recruitment professional (quality assurance)

From: David Jameson [djameson@email.com]
To: Recipient's e-mail address
Cc:
Subject: Quality Assurance Technician, Reliability, Problem solving, Attention to detail

Dear Recipient's Name,

If you are looking for a dedicated and competent Quality Assurance Technician, look no further. In 15 years' experience in quality assurance and quality control I have designed better consumer-friendly products and improved sales of existing products. Reliability, problem solving, attention to detail and focus are a few of the qualities I bring to Quality Assurance work.

Delivering solid productivity increases has been the norm throughout my career in the electronics field. I have achieved superior results with ABC Biomedical, DEF Technologies, WHI Electronics, JKL Healthcare, MNO Magnetic and PQR Electronics.

My track record means your client gets a Quality Assurance Technician who is productive from day one. My commitment would be to simplify processes, improve products, develop workforce competencies, and boost output while completing projects ahead of time and under budget.

Further qualifications are outlined in the attached CV. Given my technical skills, familiarity with the product line, and understanding of electronics manufacturing, I could step into the position and be of immediate assistance.

Please contact me by phone or e-mail to arrange a convenient time to meet. Thank you for your time; I look forward to speaking to you soon.

Yours sincerely

David Jameson
0123456 7890
Attachment: CV

Direct approach to a recruitment professional (executive computer specialist)

From: Kelly Hillman [kehillman@email.com]
To: Recipient's e-mail address
Cc:
Subject: Executive Computer Specialist job posting

Dear Recipient's Name,

My experience installing and maintaining computer networks, hardware and software, along with my skills in training users and developing cost-saving applications, are the assets I would bring to the position of Executive Computer Specialist.

I am a Certified Novell Administrator. And my technical skills include expertise in Novell Netware, MS DOS and Windows, as well as experience with hardware including Cabletron, and software including the Microsoft Office Suite.

My computer expertise has saved my employers production time and costs. As a Senior Computer Specialist, I:

- Installed a Personal Computer LAN using the Novell Netware Networking System. I saved £35,000 and used the savings to upgrade the equipment installation.

- Designed and implemented a system to cut printing costs. The system is projected to save the government £4 million over four years.

- Developed software packages, including 'point of sale' software and mortgage software, for commercial application.

I believe my skills and experience will make me succeed in the position of Executive Computer Specialist. Kindly review my CV which details my experience and achievements, and I then look forward to discussing technological solutions with you.

Yours sincerely,

Kelly Hillman
0123456 7890
Attachment: CV

Direct approach to a recruitment professional (senior executive)

From: Thomas Flokhart [tjflokhart@email.com]
To: Recipient's e-mail address
Cc:
Subject: Director Operations/Administration

Dear Recipient's Name,

In the course of your search assignments, you may have a requirement for an organized and goal-directed Senior Executive, a title I currently hold. I have a BA from _____ and an MBA from _____. Strengths that will contribute to my success in such a position include:

- direct line operations responsibility improving gross margin to 8.0 per cent;
- planning and developing over £15 million in new construction projects;
- reduction of departmental operating expenses to 1.1 per cent below budget;
- negotiating and developing contractual arrangements with vendors.

I have the ability to define problems, assess both large-scale and smaller implications of a project, and implement solutions.

The attached CV outlines my administrative and business background. My geographic preferences are the central and South East regions of the country. Relocating to a client's location does not present a problem. Also, I possess a degree from _____ University, and a BA in Business Administration from _____ University. Depending upon location and other factors, my salary requirements would be between £130,000 and £150,000.

If it appears that my qualifications meet the needs of one of your clients, I will be happy to discuss my background further.

Yours sincerely,

Thomas Flokhart
0123456 7890
Attachment: CV

Direct approach to a recruitment professional (senior manager)

From: Lisa Botkin [lbotkin@email.com]
To: Recipient's e-mail address
Cc:
Subject: Senior Executive – Finance

Dear Recipient's Name,

Mentored by Bob _____, founder of _____, I successfully progressed within his privately held organization for 12 years, serving on the **Board of Directors of 13 separate companies** and holding positions including **Treasurer, Head of Finance,** and ultimately **CEO**. During my tenure the company grew from seven employees to more than 1,000 while **revenues increased from £3 million to £108 million**. My attached CV gives further detail.

I have built my career on my commitment and ability to create open lines of communication between the Board of Directors and senior management to **protect the investments of my organization and to assure the attainment of the target return**. I have the experience, talent and energy to turn around, create, or develop a dynamic organization.

I am interested in exploring any senior management opportunities that may be available through your organization and would also be interested in interim or consulting roles. Geographically speaking, I have no limitations and am available for relocation throughout the UK and abroad.

I look forward to hearing from you in the near future to discuss any mutually beneficial opportunities.

Yours sincerely,

Lisa Botkin
01234 567890
Attachment: CV

Direct approach to a recruitment professional (international operations)

From: Franklin Townsend [frtownsend@email.com]
To: Recipient's e-mail address
Cc:
Subject: International Operations and Project Management

Dear Recipient's Name,

Over 12 years, I have built a successful career in **international operations and project management**. I have extensive experience in **diplomacy and international public affairs** dealing with foreign government officials, Heads of State, and Ambassadors as well as FTSE 100 senior executives. I am particularly adept at living and working effectively in foreign countries with diverse cultural imperatives.

Feasibility studies, crisis resolution and international risk assessment are areas where I excel. Unit construction and operations, mining/drilling and industrial equipment procurement, and sales and distribution are areas where I may be of particular assistance, but my skills are transferable to virtually any industry.

I look forward to hearing from you to discuss any mutually beneficial opportunities that you may be aware of. Please feel free to send my CV to others who may have a need for a professional of my calibre. I am willing to explore interim assignments and consulting projects as well as senior management opportunities. My attached CV details some of my accomplishments and credentials.

Yours sincerely,

Franklin Townsend
01234 567890
Attachment: CV

Direct approach to a recruitment professional (IT professional)

From: Jacqueline Smith [smithITpro@mindspring.com]
To: Recipient's e-mail address
Cc:
Subject: IT design and implementation

Dear Recipient's Name,

Capitalizing on my success managing IT design and implementation projects for ABC Design in Anytown, I am seeking a professional opportunity where my project management, customer relations and organizational skills can benefit your clients.

Some of the skills and experience I would bring to the position include:

- *defining project parameters, including interviewing clients to assess goals and objectives, and developing specifications and project deliverables;*
- *serving on leadership teams that have managed project budgets of up to £10 million to consistently meet customer timeline requirements and budgetary constraints;*
- *coordinating activities of programmers, web developers, software engineers, network engineers, graphic artists and customer representatives to meet project goals;*
- *testing and validating applications during development stages and upon completion to ensure client objectives are met.*

I am open to relocation anywhere in the United Kingdom and would eagerly accept either contract assignments or permanent employment. Thank you for your time and consideration and please review my attached CV. I look forward to speaking to you soon.

Yours sincerely,

Jacqueline Smith
1234 5678901
Attachment: CV

Direct approach to a recruitment professional (computer professional)

From: Sally Winston [computerpro@earthlink.net]
To: Recipient's e-mail address
Cc:
Subject: Technology guru with business development and global experience

Dear Recipient's Name,

My broad background in all aspects of computers, from design and installation to user training and maintenance, coupled with my business operations expertise, are the assets I would bring to a position with one of your clients.

Currently, I hold a management level position with ABC Graphics, a firm that designs and builds flight simulators for UK and foreign governments. I provide the electronics expertise in completing approximately 12 major projects annually, which means I conceptualize the simulators' computerized mechanisms, direct the design and manufacturing processes, then install and test the systems at clients' sites around the globe.

The other major aspect of my job involves aggressively targeting new business. At a point when ABC was facing an essentially saturated UK market, I designed and implemented an internet website to target international clientele. The site generated 80 per cent of our new business within one year.

Other assets I would bring to one of your clients include skill in relocating entire company IT systems, as well as experience servicing all major brands of PCs. I am familiar with nearly every computer-associated component, program or operating system on today's market.

Thank you in advance for taking a few moments to review my attached CV. I am confident that the experience you'll find outlined therein will be valuable to your clients. I look forward to hearing from you.

Yours sincerely,

Sally Winston
12345 678901
Attachment: CV

Direct approach to a recruitment professional (programmer/analyst)

From: Suresh Gupta [certifiedprogrammer@yahoo.com]
To: Recipient's e-mail address
Cc:
Subject: Programmer Analyst

Dear Recipient's Name,

My certification in computer programming, along with my professional background in electro-mechanical engineering, are among the primary assets I would bring to a programmer/analyst position with one of your clients who specialize in website development.

As part of my training at the Computer Institute in South London, I designed, wrote, edited and modified numerous e-commerce websites. These projects succeeded not only because of my skill in applying my technical knowledge, but also because of my strict attention to detail and understanding of computer architecture, fostered by my 6 years of engineering experiences.

Currently I'm employed at ABC Pharmaceuticals in Lincoln, executing experiments on electrical/mechanical equipment I was involved in manufacturing to ensure conformance to customers' specifications.

I am committed to continuing my professional education, and success as a programmer analyst. I love the work. Please review my attached CV. I look forward to hearing from you to arrange an interview.

Yours sincerely,

Suresh Gupta
12345 678901
Attachment: CV

Direct approach to a recruitment professional (IT management)

From: Maria Costas [ITexpert@anyserver.co.uk]
To: Recipient's e-mail address
Cc:
Subject: IT Management, needs/evaluations/vendors/systems development/beta/quality/
         documentation/multisite

Dear Recipient's Name,

Information technology projects for high-growth companies is my area of expertise. Throughout my career I have been successful in identifying organizational needs and leading the development and implementation of industry-specific technologies to improve productivity, quality, operating performance and profitability.

Responsibilities include the entire project management cycle, from initial needs assessment and technology evaluations through vendor selection, internal systems development, beta testing, quality review, technical and user documentation, and full-scale, multi-site implementation.

In my current position at XYZ Company, I initiated and managed the technological advances, administrative infrastructures, training programmes, and customization initiatives that have enabled the company to generate over £3 million in additional profits in the past year.

My technological and management talents are complemented by my strong training, leadership and customer service skills. I am accustomed to providing ongoing support and relate well with employers at all levels of an organization. Most notable are my strengths in facilitating cooperation among cross-functional project teams to ensure that all projects are delivered on time, within budget, and as per specifications.

Originally hired for a one-year contract at XYZ Company, I have been offered a permanent position within the company. However, I am interested in greater challenges and would welcome the opportunity to meet you to determine the contributions I can make to your client. My CV is attached and I will call you next week to set up an appointment.

Yours sincerely,

Maria Costas
12345 678910
Attachment: CV

Direct approach to a recruitment professional (systems integration)

From: Michael Wilson [systemsintegrationpro@hotmail.com]
To: Recipient's e-mail address
Cc:
Subject: Systems Integration job posting, software, firmware and hardware

Dear Recipient's Name,

My 14 years in electrical engineering supported by extensive management and product development experience are key assets that I can contribute to your client's future success. I can contribute significant expertise in systems integration within the telecommunications industry.

I work with cutting-edge technologies, including **embedded microprocessors, RF, telecommunications,** and **wireless,** in the development and manufacture of products for varied industries. Integrating software, firmware and hardware to create unique applications is a key strength. Applications that proved quite marketable include custom instrumentation and a PC-based network for GPS-tracking vehicles in transit. In addition, I have also played an important role in both the sales and customer support process, helping ABC win its largest municipal contract with the City of London.

I welcome the opportunity to meet you to explore areas of mutual benefit. Attached is my CV for your review. In order to present my credentials more fully, I will follow up with a call to you to answer any questions you may have. Thank you for your consideration.

Yours sincerely,

Michael Wilson
12345 678910
Attachment: CV

Direct approach to a recruitment professional (senior marketing executive)

From: Joshua Michaels [marketingexec@yahoo.com]
To: Recipient's e-mail address
Cc:
Subject: Ref: Your Marketing Executive Search

Dear Recipient's Name,

I recently learned that you have a Marketing Director assignment in process. I am a serious candidate for this position. Please consider:

- After joining _____ as Marketing Director, I revitalized a declining processed-meats product category in less than a year, introducing better-tasting formulas and actually reducing product costs by over £100,000. Dramatic new packaging enhanced appetite appeal, and fresh promotion strategies doubled previous sales records.

- I have carefully crafted and fine-tuned many new product introductions and line extensions, such as _____ turkey, _____ processed meats, and _____'s deodorant.

- My sales/marketing experience dates from 200–, when I formed a direct sales company to pay for my _____ MBA. Much of my subsequent success springs from strong working relationships with sales management and joint sales calls with field reps and marketing executives. I have designed events like the _____ programme, and _____'s sponsorship of the motorsports racing team.

- I have a strong personal and professional interest in consumer electronics. I consult professionally and have successfully adapted marketing techniques for home and commercial satellite systems, 'high-tech' audio/video, and radio communications equipment.

I am fluent in French and quickly absorb other languages. If this interests you, please review my attached CV and give me a call.

Yours sincerely,

Joshua Michaels
12345 678910
Attachment: CV

Direct approach to a recruitment professional (logistics)

From: Leonard Curtis [logisticspro@earthlink.net]
To: Recipient's e-mail address
Cc:
Subject: A logical choice for your client

Dear Recipient's Name,

An industry association referred to your organization as an active and selective executive search firm because of your work in logistics. I liked that referral and think my experience might be of interest.

I have a seven-year career using logistics to cut costs and improve profits, usually in concert with other parts of the business. For example:

- I supervised the start-up of several remote offices to assist our plants in improving their distribution operations. By offering customized service, and through sharp negotiations, we saved over £500 million in various operations and warehouse costs.

- I directed the efforts of sizable computer resources in the design and installation of a major application that saved £2.5 million in carrier costs. The application became the standard throughout the company's 46 locations.

- Working with International Sales, I have established various Quality Control programmes that have improved the timeliness and accuracy of product and paperwork delivery. Customer complaints plummeted to virtually zero, and remain there today.

A recent reorganization has reduced the number of senior management positions available within my company. I have concluded that another firm may offer a position and career advancement more in line with my personal expectations.

Please see my attached CV. I would like to talk to you further. I suggest next week, the week of 29 October, if you have a free minute. I look forward to hearing from you.

Yours sincerely,

Leonard Curtis
12345 678910
Attachment: CV

Direct approach to a recruitment professional (head of asset liquidation)

From: Gene Harrison [assetliquidationpro@mindspring.com]
To: Recipient's e-mail address
Cc:
Subject: Asset liquidation challenge? Get this guy!

Dear Recipient's Name,

As the Head of Lease Asset Liquidation with XYZ Ltd, I successfully engineered the recovery of £23 million in assets, almost three times the original buyout offer of £8 million.

Throughout my career I have been instrumental in developing and implementing workout and liquidation strategies and as such I have earned a strong reputation as a professional who gets the job done.

My reason for contacting you is simple. I am interested in project opportunities that will serve both to challenge and to use my abilities in asset liquidation management. My current project will be completed within the next four to six weeks. I am currently considering offers and intend to make a decision by 1st February.

The attached CV details some of my accomplishments. I look forward to hearing from you to discuss any mutually beneficial opportunities.

Yours sincerely,

Gene Harrison
12345 678910
Attachment: CV

Direct approach to a recruitment professional (systems administration)

From: Your Name [Your e-mail address]
To: Recipient's e-mail address
Cc:
Subject: Sys admin/people skills/military background

Dear Recipient's Name,

If you seek a new Systems Administrator who is technically proficient and has verifiable interpersonal skills, then we have good reason to talk. Whatever the Sys Admin challenge, I've done it, done it under fire, and can handle whatever you throw at me; that's my military training speaking.

I possess extensive technical skills and experience. My primary focus has been on Windows NT. In fact, I am currently pursuing my Microsoft Certified Systems Engineer designation. My plans are to attain this at about the time I leave the army in two months, when I will be able to bring this added expertise to an employer. My attached CV has all the details.

More difficult to portray on a CV are people skills. My job is to serve as a support person, there to keep the system operating smoothly for end-users, as well as to provide training. Colleagues, supervisors, subordinates, and end-users will confirm my interpersonal skills.

Sys Admin is a team and cross-functional team effort. I have commendations for my abilities as a team player as well as a team leader and a verifiable track record in taking projects and running with them, but the successes are a result of the combined efforts of the whole team.

A meeting would be greatly appreciated. I look forward to speaking with you in the near future. Please review my attached CV.

Yours sincerely,

Your Name
0123456 7890
Attachment: CV

Direct approach to a recruitment professional (sales manager)

From: Your Name [Your e-mail address]
To: Recipient's e-mail address
Cc:
Subject: Sales management that delivers on commitments

Dear Recipient's Name,

If you have a client seeking a top-performing Sales Management Professional with cross-functional expertise in account management, business development, and sales training, I offer a progressive track record of combining big-picture strategic market planning with tenacity in setting and achieving goals, building relationships, and motivating and energizing sales teams at all levels.

Representative of my accomplishments are:

- As Senior Account Manager, I built a national account base from £8.5 million to £11 million for a leading pet food company, working with industry-leading retailers such as ABC, XYZ and DEF. I trained and led the top-performing sales team in the country and have been the recipient of numerous industry awards for top sales and market growth.
- I developed marketing plans for a £2 million region – consisting of 150 wholesalers across the UK for GHI. For four consecutive years I increased regional sales an average of £250K.
- Previously, as Northwest Regional Manager for JKL, I achieved the highest sales increases – up to 46 per cent – in the company.

I am strong in collaborative sales and demonstrate powerful results in working with customers to help them excel in highly competitive markets. Using an innate sense of market and consumer needs, as well as strong analytical and forecasting skills, I offer a proven record of delivering sales increases, building account bases, and training internal and external teams across diverse consumer products categories.

While my attached CV provides an overview of my past performance, I would welcome a meeting to discuss your needs and my ability to become a contributing member of your team. I look forward to talking to you.

Yours sincerely,

Your Name
0123456 7890
Attachment: CV

Direct approach to a recruitment professional (senior enterprise/IT architect)

From: Your Name [Your e-mail address]
To: Recipient's e-mail address
Cc:
Subject: IT Architect enhances infrastructures, systems, and processes

Dear Recipient's Name,

As a Senior Enterprise/IT Architect with a track record of enhancing infrastructures, systems, and processes for world-class organizations, I think my skills should be of interest to one of your clients.

As a PMP-certified IT professional with _____ for the past ten years, I have driven and contributed to major technology initiatives that have been critical to supporting company growth. I offer a proven track record of consistent, on-time, fully functional delivery of challenging IT projects. For example:

- Formulated architecture road maps by instituting standards, developing architecture tools, and developing IT governance foundations for numerous high-impact projects.
- Established architectural standards and selected technologies that fully met current needs while providing a sound infrastructure to support _____ 's future enterprise needs.

Although I have had a rewarding career with _____ , I am currently seeking a new professional challenge. My attached CV will provide an overview of my credentials, and hopefully lead to conversation and a personal meeting at which we can discuss your needs and my ability to contribute.

Yours sincerely,

Your Name
0123456 7890
Attachment: CV

Direct approach to a recruitment professional (senior network control technician)

From: Your Name [Your e-mail address]
To: Recipient's e-mail address
Cc:
Subject: Senior Network Control Technician job posting

Dear Recipient's Name,

I am excited by your job posting for Senior Network Control Technician/Administrator. My qualifications and technical background, as well as fieldwork, marketing, and customer service experience, match your requirements for this position. The attached CV reflects the experience and technical training needed to provide customized network and hardware and software solutions to meet remote customer needs.

I believe the following are relevant to your needs:

- An accommodating attitude and willingness to work hard at any level to accomplish tasks and meet deadlines.
- The ability to multitask, prioritizing tasks and job assignments to balance customer needs with company goals.
- Strategic planning to head off downtime and restructure company systems to realize major improvement.
- Aptitude for troubleshooting problems, while respecting customers and explaining problems/ solutions in accessible language.
- Consultative, straightforward communication techniques that promote development of strong and lasting rapport and trust.
- A work ethic that honours integrity and excellence to enhance company distinction.
- A persuasive, take-charge style seasoned with a sense of humour for a pleasant work environment.
- Psychological insight and a talent for motivating others to work at higher levels to increase productivity.

An interview to investigate your needs and my qualifications further would be of great interest to your clients. I look forward to hearing from you. Thank you for your time and consideration.

Yours sincerely,

Your Name
0123456 7890
Attachment: CV

Direct approach to a recruitment professional (senior systems engineer, e-procurement)

From: Your Name [Your e-mail address]
To: Recipient's e-mail address
Cc:
Subject: Systems Engineer e-Procurement

Dear Recipient's Name,

Your Senior Systems Engineer for e-Procurement position aligns with my history of managing successful IT initiatives and complex projects from initial conception through development to successful launch. I fully understand the importance of strategy development that brings mission-critical projects in on schedule and within budget.

I have a proven record of strategic process planning, goal setting, and tactical implementation to achieve objectives. If your clients need leaders with the ability to motivate teams and individuals to new levels of effectiveness and impact, please consider my track record of:

- Providing leadership that promotes an organizational structure and culture conducive to the development of a highly motivated workforce, where initiative and commitment are essential, encouraged, and cultivated.
- Developing and executing strategies to address and resolve challenges through strategic, collaborative, and tactical approaches.
- Driving performance improvements that positively impact time, cost, quality, and delivery.

As a *critical thinker* who is skilled in developing strategic plans and procedures to optimize efficiency, reduce costs, protect assets, and maximize profitability, I am confident that I can be of significant service to one of your clients.

The attached CV, although detailed and comprehensive, does not fully demonstrate the integrity, dedication, and value I deliver. I would appreciate the opportunity to discuss possible options. I look forward to hearing from you.

Yours sincerely,

Your Name
0123456 7890
Attachment: CV

Networking e-mail
(managerial/administrative position)

A colleague to whom Maurice hasn't spoken in several months has been nominated for a prestigious award. He decides to capitalize on an opportunity to renew the acquaintance and enlist her help in his job search.

From: Maurice DuMaurier [mdumaurier@email.com]
To: Recipient's e-mail address
Cc:
Subject: Congratulations!

Dear Recipient's Name,

Congratulations on your nomination for the XYZ Award, the nomination demonstrates the high degree of professional excellence you have achieved.

It's been a while since we've chatted, and I wanted to bring you up-to-date on what I've been doing. After leaving DEF, I explored several options before accepting a position as Director of Human Resources for GHI. Unfortunately, the daily drive to Anothertown, among other factors, proved to be untenable – particularly during the winter months – and I have left that position.

This puts me back in the job market, and I am writing to inquire if you are aware of any managerial/administrative positions that would capitalize on my skills. I am flexible regarding specific job responsibilities and am most interested in making a meaningful contribution to an organization's success. With these goals in mind, I have attached an updated CV.

Reiterating some of the key capabilities that I can bring to a position, consider the following:

- **excellent team-building and leadership skills;**
- **superb interpersonal skills and supervisory experience;**
- **developing and implementing human resource policies;**
- **extensive knowledge and experience in the healthcare arena.**

I am convinced that my experience and professional diligence could be an asset to one of the IMC's members, and would appreciate any referrals you might be able to give me for potential employment opportunities. Feel free to pass my CV on to anyone who may have an appropriate opportunity, or give me a call on 12345 678901.

Thank you in advance for your much-appreciated assistance. I look forward to talking to you soon.

Yours sincerely,

Maurice DuMaurier
12345 678901
Attachment: CV

Networking e-mail (internship/employment)

This e-mail is from a Japanese exchange student pursuing either an internship or employment.

From: Motoshi Mori [mmori@email.com]
To: Recipient's e-mail address
Cc:
Subject: Internship opportunity

Dear Recipient's Name,

Since meeting you earlier this year at the Korean Film Festival we have exchanged e-mails and met several times. We have discussed our mutual interest in the Japanese film industry and its future in the global entertainment business. You know well my vision of integrating Japanese gaming and animation technologies into filmmaking.

Over the course of our conversations, you have mentioned that there might be an opportunity for an internship or, possibly, employment in the Creative Media Academy. I am very interested.

I offer negotiation, persuasion and liaison abilities and management, leadership and communication skills. I have also proven that I can use my bilingual proficiency to enhance international relations. Please see my CV for examples of how I have used these abilities in the past.

I believe that my unique strengths can contribute to the growth of the Creative Media programme, particularly if you are able to secure departmental status. I welcome the opportunity to discuss my continued involvement in your programme.

Yours sincerely,

Motoshi Mori
0123456 7890
Attachment: CV

Networking e-mail
(computer and information systems manager)

This e-mail was sent to follow up a meeting with a medical school dean.

From: David Kent [dkent@email.com]
To: Recipient's e-mail address
Cc:
Subject: Web Development

Dear Recipient's Name,

Perhaps you remember our chance meeting at the Bio Asia-Pacific Conference at the Sheraton Waikiki on 18 and 19 August 20–. In our brief conversation, I shared with you the idea of using Web Development as an administrative tool. You expressed interest in the possibility of implementing such a system within the School of Medicine.

May I suggest a formal meeting to explore the idea?

I have some exciting and creative ideas, which may encourage you to take the next step toward realizing the positive impact a content management system would have in the School of Medicine. This would also be a great opportunity for us to discuss your goals and how an administrative intranet would help you reach them in a more efficient and cost-effective manner.

In addition, there has recently been spirited discussion within the IT community on the topic of organizational continuity and its potential vulnerability due to advances in technology. I think you'll find the specific strategies I have to share with you thought provoking.

If you recall, my background is in Web Planning and Development, with specific skills in developing administrative intranets and public websites, and designing web-based software to address the internal and external reporting needs of organizations.

Please see my attached CV attesting to my experience and specialities. I will contact you within the next few days to discuss the possibility of meeting you.

Yours sincerely,

David Kent
Computer and Information Systems Manager

0123456 7890
Attachment: CV

Networking e-mail (general)

From: Linda Brown [lbrown@email.com]
To: Recipient's e-mail address
Cc:
Subject: Thanks for the advice

Dear Philip,

Congratulations on your re-election. I hope this letter finds you and your family well and that you have an enjoyable holiday.

I am writing to update you on my job search. You may recall from our last discussion that I am now focusing on obtaining a position that will sustain me until such time as I am ready for retirement (in three to five years).

As you recommended, I have applications on file with ABC for various positions and have corresponded with various department heads, in each case indicating my flexibility and strong interest in making a meaningful contribution to smooth operations within one of their departments.

Philip, I genuinely appreciate the advice and assistance you have offered to date. Once again, I am requesting that if you are aware of any other avenues I should be pursuing, please let me know. I believe I have skills and experience to offer and can be an asset to someone in just about any position requiring maturity, reliability and dedication.

Thank you, again, for all your help.

Yours sincerely,

Linda Brown

0123456 7890
Attachment: CV

Networking e-mail (HR administration)

From: Angela Sullivan [hrspecialist@hotmail.com]
To: Recipient's e-mail address
Cc:
Subject: Great to talk to you again!

Dear Recipient's Name,

It was a pleasure to speak to you on the telephone recently and, even more so, to be remembered after all these years.

As mentioned during our conversation, I have recently re-entered the job market and have 10 years' experience with a 3,000-employee retail organization in the area of human resources administration. My experience includes recruitment and selection, human resources planning and employee relations. I have been responsible for all facets of management of company personnel, including development and training, and liaison with both staff and training providers.

My goal is to become an HR Manager in a larger organization with the possibility of advancement in other Human Resources areas. My preference is to remain in the _____ area.

For your information, my CV is attached. If any situations come to mind where you think my skills and background would fit or if you have any suggestions as to others with whom it might be beneficial for me to speak, I would appreciate hearing from you. I can be reached on the telephone number shown below.

Again, I very much enjoyed our conversation.

Yours sincerely,

Angela Sullivan
0123456 7890
Attachment: CV

Networking e-mail (publishing)

From: Robert Render [publishingpro@anyserver.co.uk]
To: Recipient's e-mail address
Cc:
Subject: Thanks for all the help

Dear Recipient's Name,

It was a pleasure to meet you for lunch today. I am grateful for the time you took out of your busy schedule to assist me in my job search.

It was fascinating to learn about the new technology that is beginning to play a major role in the publishing field today. I have already been to the bookshop to purchase the book by _____ which you highly recommended. I look forward to reading about his 'space age' ideas.

I will be contacting _____ within the next few days to set up an appointment. I will let you know how things are progressing once I have met her.

Thanks again for your help. You will be hearing from me soon.

Yours sincerely,

Robert Render
012345 6789
Attachment: CV

Networking e-mail (advertising manager)

From: Your Name [Your e-mail address]
To: Recipient's e-mail address
Cc:
Subject: Let's keep in touch

Dear Recipient's Name,

It was a pleasure speaking to you Monday afternoon regarding my search for a position in Corporate Graphic Design. Thank you for your initial interest.

The position I am looking for is usually found in a corporate marketing or public relations department. The titles vary: Design Manager, Advertising Manager, and Publications Director are a few. In almost every case the job description includes management and coordination of the corporation's online and print marketing materials, whether they are produced by in-house designers or by an outside advertising agency or design firm.

I would like to stay in the area; at least, I would like to search this area first. My salary requirement currently is in the £__ ,___ range.

My professional experience, education, activities, and skills uniquely qualify me for a position in Corporate Graphic Design. My portfolio documents over eight years of experience in the business, and includes design, project consultation, and supervision of quality printed material for a wide range of clients.

I hope you will keep my CV on your files for future reference. If I come across anyone suitable to your needs, I'll certainly give you a shout.

Yours sincerely,

Your Name
0123456 7890
Attachment: CV

Networking e-mail (construction management)

From: Your Name [Your e-mail address]
To: Recipient's e-mail address
Cc:
Subject: Follow-up on Chamber of Commerce conversation

Dear Recipient's Name,

We had the opportunity to speak briefly at the Chamber of Commerce meeting last week about the Construction Management position you are seeking to fill in _____. I appreciate you filling me in on the details of the project, and I'm following up as you suggested.

As we discussed, I am well acquainted with _____'s brand and store concept, and I am excited to learn of your expansion plans. With my background in construction, maintenance, project management, and operations leadership, I believe I am primed to play a key role in this growth.

As the founder of Superior Landscape Design, I have been instrumental in leading the company to phenomenal success within a very short time, building the organization from start-up into a solid revenue generator reputed throughout the North West as an aggressive competitor in markets crowded by multi-million-pound, nationally-recognized companies.

I am currently in the process of selling the company, and have been exploring opportunities with dynamic, growth-oriented organizations like yours that could benefit from my broad-based expertise in operations, organizational management, finance, and business development. Complementing my diverse leadership background is expertise in all the fundamentals of construction management, including the ability to see projects through to completion on time and on budget.

Perhaps one of my strongest assets is my ability to cultivate long-lasting relationships with clients through attentive, direct communication. I have been highly successful at defining complex project plans, establishing budgets, outlining scope of work, and directly soliciting qualified contractors using the bid process. I also offer extensive experience navigating paperwork and bureaucracy, through which I forge productive alliances with key regulatory agencies to streamline permitting and licensing and expedite project starts.

I would welcome the opportunity to speak to you again in greater detail. Could we meet for lunch on Friday? I have attached my CV and will call your assistant in a few days to confirm a meeting.

Yours sincerely,

Your Name
0123456 7890
Attachment: CV

Networking e-mail (database administration)

From: Your Name [Your e-mail address]
To: Recipient's e-mail address
Cc:
Subject: 6 Years' Intranet implementation 15K users

Dear Recipient's Name,

Our mutual colleague, _____ _____ , suggested that I send you my CV. I am looking to make a change and he mentioned that your department is looking for a Database Administrator with experience in Intranet implementation and management.

As my attached CV demonstrates, I have done that type of work for six years with a regional organization on a platform of 15,000 users.

This sounds like exactly the kind of work I could sink my teeth into. I would welcome the opportunity to discuss my expertise in relation to the specific deliverables of your job.

After you have reviewed my CV, can we talk?

Yours sincerely,

Your Name
012345 67890
Attachment: CV

Networking e-mail (executive assistant)

From: Your Name [Your e-mail address]
To: Recipient's e-mail address
Cc:
Subject: Executive Assistant referral

Dear Recipient's Name,

I was very pleased to learn of the need for an Executive Assistant in your company from your colleague _____ _____ . I believe the qualities you seek are well matched by my track record:

Your Needs	My Qualifications
Independent Self-starter	• Served as company liaison between sales representatives, controlling commission and products.
	• Controlled cash flow, budget planning, and bank reconciliation for three companies.
	• Assisted in the promotion of a restaurant within a private placement sales effort, creating sales materials and communicating with investors.
Computer Experience	• Used Lotus Notes in preparing financial spreadsheet used in private placement memoranda and Macintosh to design brochures and flyers.
	• Have vast experience with both computer programming and the current software packages.
Compatible Background	• Spent 5 years overseas and speak French.
	• Served as an executive assistant to four corporate heads.

A CV is attached that covers my experience and qualifications in greater detail. I would appreciate the opportunity to discuss my credentials in a personal interview.

Yours sincerely,

Your Name
0123456 7890
Attachment: CV

Networking e-mail (financial professional)

From: Your Name [Your e-mail address]
To: Recipient's e-mail address
Cc:
Subject: _____ suggested I contact you re Finance Associate position

Dear Recipient's Name,

I recently spoke to ____ _____ from _____ _____ , and he strongly recommended that I send you a copy of my CV. I am very pleased to learn of the need for a **Finance Associate** and I believe the qualities you seek are well matched by my track record:

Your Needs	My Qualifications
3–5 years' experience building and maintaining complex financial models	Four years' experience at a top-performing hedge fund
	Built and maintained complex financial models to support investment theses in private equity transactions and coverage of over 30 stocks, £100 million of portfolio value
	Created matrices in Excel to analyse model sensitivity to risk factors
Background of exceptional academic performance	BSc in Economics from _____
Ability to manage multiple projects and meet deadlines	Delivered 15–20 research reports and notes per month in a fast-paced work environment

My greatest strength lies in my ability to communicate complex financial information clearly. This has enabled me to summarize the results of models and in-depth due diligence into concise investment theses for the portfolio managers of ____ _____ , resulting in many profitable investments.

I am confident that my dedication, enthusiasm, and creativity would allow me to make a real contribution to your team. I hope to converse with you further and will call the week of 2nd August to follow up.

Yours sincerely,

Your Name
01234 567890
Attachment: CV

Networking e-mail (international sales manager)

From: Your Name [Your e-mail address]
To: Recipient's e-mail address
Cc:
Subject: International Sales Manager referral

Dear Recipient's Name:

I was recently talking to _____ _____ from your company and he strongly recommended that I send you a copy of my CV in reference to the above position. Knowing the requirements, he felt that I would be an ideal candidate. For more than eleven years, I have been involved in international sales management, with seven years directly in the aerospace industry. My qualifications for the position include:

- Establishing sales offices in France, Great Britain, and Germany.
- Recruiting and managing a group of 24 international sales representatives.
- Providing training programmes for all of the European staff, which included full briefing on our own products as well as competitor lines.
- Obtaining 42 per cent, 33 per cent, and 31 per cent of the French, German, and British markets, respectively.
- Dealing with all local engine and airframe manufacturers.
- Generating more than £32 million in sales with excellent margins.

My BSc in electrical engineering was obtained from the University of _____ and my languages include French and German.

I feel confident that an interview would demonstrate my expertise in setting up rep organizations, and training and managing an international sales department; given my interest in your company, this could be time well spent. I look forward to meeting you and will give you a call to follow up on this letter the week of _____ .

My CV is attached for your review.

Yours sincerely,

Your Name
01234 567890
Attachment: CV

Networking e-mail via LinkedIn (career change)

LinkedIn.com networking letters

LinkedIn is the leading social networking site for professionals. At LinkedIn, all communications to other members are sent through the site, so every letter has a similar format. As social networking sites exist for people to communicate and reach out to each other, you will notice that these letters, while polite and professional, cut right to the chase.

If you know someone, or have known him or her in the past, you simply send a request to link. This will probably be fairly limited, so you will need to reach out to others that you don't know. The two easiest ways to do this are:

1   Send a request to link through someone you know to the person you would like to know; the site automatically shows you the people who can provide the patch for your introduction.

2   You can join special interest groups: There are hundreds, maybe thousands. Then as a member of a group, you can approach any other member directly for a link, based on your mutual membership of that group.

Here are a few examples of networking letters to and from members of the LinkedIn social networking site.

_____ _____ has sent you a message.
Date: **/**/2015
Subject: FOOD TRUMPS PHARMACEUTICALS

Dear _____ :

I have a passion for food. I want to move from the pharma industry, where I am a Brand Manager for _____ , to the food and beverage industry. I recently heard about a position as an Associate Brand Manager at _____ and see considerable similarity in the brand strategies.

I know that I can make an immediate and long-term contribution to _____ . I would love to send you my CV and, if you like what you see (and I believe you will), perhaps we can set up time to speak live.

Regards,

Your Name
0123456 7890
you@email.com

Networking e-mail via LinkedIn
(to a member of a common interest group)

_____ _____ has sent you a message.

Date: **/**/2015

Subject: Exchange leads?

Hello _____ ,

I came across your profile on LinkedIn while doing a job search here on LI. We're both part of the SharePoint Experts Group, and thought it might make sense to connect. Let me know if I can be of assistance in your networking efforts here on LI. Perhaps we could talk and exchange leads?

Sincerely,

Your Name
0123456 7890
you@email.com

Networking e-mail via LinkedIn
(introduction request)

___ ____ has sent you a message.

Date: **/**/2015

Subject: Connection request

_____Congratulations on your new job! It's always good to see friends moving onwards and upwards. I noticed from your LinkedIn profile that you are now connected with _____ , and I wonder whether you can make a LinkedIn introduction or send me her e-mail address. Your assistance is much appreciated; I hope I can return the favour someday soon.

Regards,

Your Name
0123456 7890
you@email.com

Networking e-mail via LinkedIn (introduction request)

This is a networking letter asking a networking contact at LinkedIn for an introduction to a prominent headhunter, a member of the recipient's network.

___ ____has sent you a message
Date: **/**/2015
Subject: Introduction request

Hi Martin,

I hope things are well. There is a gentleman named ___ _____that you are connected to on LinkedIn. ___ _____recruits for the types of jobs that I am looking at, so I was wondering if you could perhaps introduce me to him. If so, I can send a LinkedIn introduction request.

Thank you.

Your Name
0123456 7890
you@email.com

Networking e-mail via LinkedIn (endorsement request)

At LinkedIn you can ask people to endorse your work. Here is an example of an endorsement request.

___ ____ has sent you a message.
Date: **/**/2015
Subject: Can you endorse me?

Dear ___ ____,

I'm sending this to ask you for a brief recommendation of my work that I can include in my LinkedIn profile. If you have any questions, let me know.

Thanks in advance for helping me out. If you have any questions please just call or e-mail.

Regards,

Your Name
0123456 7890
you@email.com

Networking e-mail via LinkedIn (approach to a potential employer)

The following networking letter is a direct approach to a LinkedIn contact at a target company, using some good background information.

___ ____ has sent you a message.
Date: **/**/2015
Subject: Risk mitigation–related question

Dear Jacqueline,

I was very impressed with what I learned about the _____ programme in _____ at the Export-Import Bank Conference in _____ last week. That is why I write. I am interested in, among other things, risk mitigation and energy supplies and sources. I was impressed with your company's work from exactly this perspective.

I am happy to think that the move toward solar and wind is going to give the world not just better and more cost-effective power but also safer power. This is very important. At the Export-Import Bank Conference, for example, delegates from Morocco asked the Secretary for Energy if the UK would work with Morocco to do alternative energy in the south of Morocco and to include Mauritania, and, signally, to include a consortium of universities to do all of this.

I know that this is absolutely critical for Morocco and for the country's relationship with the UK and for Morocco's security with respect to the rest of Africa.

The Secretary for Energy was happy to hear Morocco wants to come to the table to do business in the south of Morocco for alternative energy sources.

All of this is my way of saying that I would like to come up to _____, to explore and learn more. It might be possible to do a write-up for a broader audience that could feature what you are doing, and we might discuss what sort of audience when we meet.

I look forward to hearing from you soon.

Regards,

Your Name
0123456 7890
you@email.com

Networking e-mail via LinkedIn (to a recruiter)

___ ____ has sent you a message.
Date: **/**/2015
Subject: NBI Certified

Dear _____,

____ _____ recommended that I contact you. I'm a senior-level staffing and recruitment professional who is seeking an opportunity in the greater Manchester area. While I am in play with a few companies right now, I'd appreciate your insight into the local market and players. In this respect, I'm hoping we might chat.

Sincerely,

Your Name
01234 567890
you@email.com

Follow-up e-mail (after telephone contact) (fundraising consultant)

From an applicant who has had too many jobs in too few years, this letter was designed to get two competing 'partners' to bring her on board.

From: Lanina Crowne [lcrowne@email.com]
To: Recipient's e-mail address
Cc:
Subject: Fundraising Consultant meeting

Dear Recipient's Name,

Thank you for making time to explore how I could help ABC & Associates as your newest Fundraising Consultant.

I've already started thinking about how I might be most productive – right from the start. Of course, my ideas must be preliminary; I don't know exactly how your organization works. Nevertheless, in response to your observations I would value your reactions to these preliminary thoughts:

- Clients need to see the tailored solutions we provide as a rapid, seamless, continuing operation that guides them through the complex world of modern fundraising.
- We need to position and brand the company as their 'sole source' for the resources they must have to grow financially and operationally.

I am modifying my continuing professional development programme to concentrate on fundraising from a consultant's perspective; this is where I see the future. I am looking through the literature and contacting professional organizations to hear about the latest trends directly from industry leaders. I'll use what I learn to re-evaluate my own successes in campaigns done with and without consultants.

I appreciate your vote of confidence in recommending that I meet Ms O'Neill. I want to make that interview just as useful for her as possible. Toward that end, may I call in a few days to get your reactions to the preliminary thoughts I've outlined above?

With many thanks for all your help…

Yours sincerely,

Lanina Crowne
01234 567890

Follow-up e-mail (after telephone contact) (legal secretary)

From: James Penson [jpenson@email.com]
To: Recipient's e-mail address
Cc:
Subject: Re our conversation about the office administration job

Dear Recipient's Name,

Thank you for returning my telephone call yesterday. It was a pleasure speaking to you, and as promised, a copy of my CV is attached. I have been working in law firms since the end of February, as well as working at weekends and in the evenings for over one year. At present, I am looking for a second or third shift to continue developing my word-processing and legal skills.

I have developed strong office skills over the years. While I was attending college, I worked as Administrative Assistant to the Department Head, in addition to working in other professional capacities.

_____ speaks very highly of me, and if you need to confirm a reference with him, please feel free to contact him at _____. In addition, I would be happy to furnish you with names of people I have worked for in law firms over the past year.

Within the next few days, I will contact you to arrange a convenient meeting time to discuss the position you now have available.

Thank you again for calling yesterday. I look forward to meeting you in person.

Yours sincerely,

James Penson
0123456 7890
Attachment: CV

Follow-up letter (after telephone contact) (manager)

Andrew T Bestwick
1 Any Street
Anytown AA1 1AA
12345 678910
managerpro@anyserver.co.uk

(Date)

Bob _____
(Title)
A,B&C
Executive Search Consultants
111 Any Avenue
Anytown AA1 1AA

Dear Mr _____,

THANK YOU for allowing me to tell you a little about myself this morning.

I offer: 10 years' operations management experience; the ABILITY to manage, build, and quickly understand their business; EXPERIENCE in domestic and international corporate cultures; INTELLIGENCE and the capacity to grasp essential elements; and the WILLINGNESS to work hard, travel and relocate.

I have just completed my MBA (December 20–) and would appreciate the opportunity to talk to your client companies that are in need of an experienced and seasoned manager. Whether the need is for general (operational) management, products, marketing or sales, my substantial background in management, marketing, and technical products should be very valuable to your clients.

Realizing that most of your clients aren't looking for Directors, I'm not necessarily looking for fancy titles (but I am promotable). What I am looking for is that special position that will offer not only a challenge but a career opportunity with long-range potential.

I will be happy to discuss details with you once you have had time to review the enclosed CV.

May we work together?

Yours sincerely,

Andrew Bestwick

Andrew Bestwick

Enclosure: CV

Follow-up e-mail (after telephone contact) (general)

From: James Young [jyoung@earthlink.net]
To: Recipient's e-mail address
Cc:
Subject: Glad we finally caught up

Dear Recipient's Name,

I appreciate the time you took yesterday to discuss the position at _____.
I recognize that timing and awareness of interest are very important in searches of this type.
Your comment regarding an attempt to contact me earlier this summer is a case in point.

Attached, as you requested, you will find my CV. My experiences as a director of client services are readily transferable to a new environment and I believe that I can contribute a great deal to the satisfaction of your client's needs.

Realizing that letters and CVs are not an entirely satisfactory means of judging a person's ability or personality, I suggest a personal interview to discuss further your client's needs and my qualifications. I can be reached directly or via message on 12345 678910, so that we can arrange a mutually convenient time to meet. I look forward to hearing from you. Thank you for your time and consideration.

Yours sincerely,

James Young
12345 678910
Attachment: CV

Follow-up e-mail (after telephone contact) (event manager)

From: Your Name [Your e-mail address]
To: Recipient's e-mail address
Cc:
Subject: Our daybreak Event Management conversation

Dear Recipient's Name,

I was lucky to catch you at the office so early yesterday morning; my day always gets off to an early start. As you will remember, we discussed, and you asked me to send you my CV in reference to, the Events Management job.

I am a fanatic about planning, execution, attention to quality and detail, and their cumulative result: communication of an image and feeling that appears effortless to event attendees.

I have never held a 'nine-to-five' job and would most likely be bored to death if I had one. It's why I find event management such a fulfilling challenge to my grey matter. I am in my element when I am in a position to organize . . . the more details the better! I have the tenacity of a terrier when it comes to achieving the impossible.

Please review my attached CV. I'll give you a buzz on Tuesday 14 March, hopefully to arrange a meeting. Call or e-mail sooner if your schedule permits; I can make the time at short notice now the annual convention is wrapped. I am looking forward to our meeting in the very near future.

Yours sincerely,

Your Name
0123456 7890
Attachment: CV

Follow-up e-mail (after telephone contact) (investment management)

From: Your Name [Your e-mail address]
To: Recipient's e-mail address
Cc:
Subject: Tchunamke/Smith quantitative analysis conversion: growth, value, investment analysis, portfolio measurement, risk control

Dear Recipient's Name,

Thank you for taking time to speak to me today. Your firm's reputation within the investment management industry prompted my call, and I am happy to learn that you have an active search that might fit my profile.

Working as a Quantitative Analyst at _____ over the past four years, I have gained valuable experience and solid skills that may be an asset, especially with a client such as _____ :

- Strong background in growth, value, and quantitative investment strategies.
- Experience in measuring portfolios against various benchmarks.
- Polished communication skills with portfolio managers.
- Quantitative risk control of portfolios.
- Passion for markets and for finding investment solutions for institutional clients.

To focus my skills in quantitative investment analysis, I recently graduated from the University of _____ with an MSc in Financial Mathematics.

I would like to discuss with you this or any other similar positions that call for my background and expertise. I look forward to hearing from you about suitable opportunities.

Yours sincerely,

Your Name
01234 567890
Attachment: CV

Follow-up e-mail (after face-to-face meeting) (loan processor)

Richard had to overcome the effects of a prolonged slowdown in his industry – portfolio management – and convince the decision-maker that his skills were transferable and he could master the intricacies of new product lines he had never worked with before.

From: Richard Weigman [rweigman@email.com]
To: Recipient's e-mail address
Cc:
Subject: Follow-up, yesterday's 2pm Loan Processor interview

Dear Recipient's Name,

Thank you for meeting me yesterday afternoon. I think ABC Mortgage Lending and I are a good match for each other. I want to become your newest loan processor team member.

In fact, as I was driving back to Anytown, I began to plan how I might be productive for you right from the start. My ideas are, of course, preliminary. But I would value your reactions to this tentative plan:

- I would start by introducing myself to every client. I want them to think of me as ABC Mortgage Lending, and I want to find out what their special needs are before any rush requirements come up. When they need answers, I want them to remember three things: my name, my phone number and my e-mail.

- I have already started my plan to master your requirements. As a first step, I'm jotting down the kinds of questions I must have the answers to so I can process loans quickly and right the first time. I want ABC Mortgage to be the 'provider of choice' in the eyes of buyers and agents – in short, anyone who wants quality loan processing services. If I am successful, I hope our percentage of revenue for mortgage loan processing grows steadily.

As you asked me to, I plan to call you on Friday. I've already thought of the question I would most like to ask. Here it is: Will the plan I've outlined work for ABC Mortgage faster and better than any plan suggested by the other candidates you've interviewed?

Yours sincerely,

Richard Weigman
0123456 7890

Follow-up e-mail (after face-to-face meeting) (hospitality manager)

Lacking professional experience, Olivia was sure to remind her interviewers of her related volunteer work, enthusiasm, education, international travel experience and multilingual communication skills.

From: Olivia Copperfield [obcopperfield@email.com]
To: Recipient's e-mail address
Cc:
Subject: Hospitality Manager meeting 6/7/15

Dear Recipient's Name,

Thank you for the opportunity to participate in a follow-up interview with you and your supervising managers, Mr Sean Johnson and Mrs Rita Bronson, to discuss further the possibility of my joining your hospitality team as Hospitality Manager.

As we discussed, ABC Hotel is the ideal work environment for me to express my enthusiasm for working with people and to put to use my education in psychology and business administration.

I feel strongly that my volunteer work experience at XYZ and my personal experience acquired over the years while travelling worldwide will prove especially valuable in this highly visible position. These things, combined with an ability to communicate effectively in Spanish, French and Italian, would allow me to make an immediate contribution.

Please note that my availability is immediate. If you need to contact me, I can be reached at the telephone number below. Thank you again for your time and consideration. I hope to speak to you soon.

Yours sincerely,

Olivia Beth Copperfield
012345 67890

Follow-up e-mail (after face-to-face meeting) (merchandise manager)

This thank-you e-mail capitalizes on reinforcing the 'fit' between the potential job and her qualifications, as well as introducing some areas overlooked in the interview.

From: Deborah Devereaux [ddevereaux@email.com]
To: Recipient's e-mail address
Cc:
Subject: Re our Merchandiser meeting

Dear Recipient's Name,

Thank you for the opportunity to be interviewed for the **Merchandise Manager** position. You were extremely generous with your time and I was impressed with the warmth and efficiency of your office, and your genuine interest in acquainting me with the company's concepts and goals.

My background is unique – it does not fit into a traditional career mould – yet it encompasses a very diverse exposure to Home Furnishings and Ready-to-Wear. As we discussed, my extensive experience with the type of clientele your company targets has prepared me to 'come on board' your team. My sales record of £279,000 (20–) demonstrates that I can produce immediate value, as well as train new sales reps in highly effective merchandising and closing techniques.

What I did not stress is that I also have built an arsenal of skills around quantitative, technical processes involved in merchandising and planning. For example, I have developed six-month merchandising plans for the London division of XYZ Apparel, and classification planning that established the focus on merchandise categories, prices, styles, sizes and colours.

I have always striven to achieve high-quality results by knowing the customer well, anticipating profitable market trends and never forgetting the store image. Offering wide, but well-edited, assortments of multiple classifications so that one-stop shopping can easily occur has been my hallmark. High standards have been central in all of my work, whether with a major retail department store, wholesale showroom or upmarket home furnishings boutique. Your corporate environment and company goals appear to reflect those same high standards, and I am eager to join your team.

Thanks again for the opportunity to attend the interview. I hope you see the match as clearly as I do.

Yours sincerely,

Deborah Devereaux
0123456 7890

Follow-up letter (after face-to-face meeting) (manufacturer representative)

Anthony Ruggerio

1 Any Street   **Anytown AA1 1AA**

Home Phone: 12345 678910 • Mobile: 0198765 4321

28 February 20–

Ms Kathleen McMann
General Manager
ABC Imaging
111 Any Avenue
Anytown AA1 1AA

Dear Ms McMann,

Thank you for the interview with you on Friday, 23rd February, for the Manufacturer's Representative position. Everything I learned from you about ABC Imaging leads me to believe that this is a progressive company where I could fully use my skills and make a valuable contribution. In fact, I have not been this determined or excited about a job since I started my business 25 years ago.

As I mentioned to you, I am sales orientated and have a solid technical background in printing. I relate well to printers at any level, from pressmen to owners. In my sales activities with John Watkins when he was a printing buyer at XYZ Industries, I found him to be very demanding and hard to please. One of the reasons why I was successful in acquiring and retaining his business was my constant commitment to customer service. Whenever there were any questions, I never failed to answer them promptly.

During our discussion, you seemed to express a concern about my lack of experience with dealers. Although I had not mentioned it, I have had long-term relationships with dealers like DEF, and have bought approximately £1 million worth of equipment from them, starting with my first press and expanding to 20 over the years. I am certain that with my persistence and follow-through I can handle dealers at the sales and service end.

Among my major strengths, I am goal-driven, self-motivated, have a strong work ethic and an ability to learn quickly. My training period would be brief, and I would use my own time to familiarize myself with your equipment and product line. In addition, I am accustomed to long hours and have no objection to the travel requirements or being away from home four days a week.

Coming from a medium-sized company, it would be an honour to work at ABC Imaging.

I look forward to talking to you again.

Yours sincerely,

Anthony Ruggerio

Follow-up e-mail (after face-to-face meeting) (general)

From: Marcy Smith [msmith@email.com]
To: Recipient's e-mail address
Cc:
Subject: Follow-up, today's 3pm meeting

Dear Recipient's Name,

Thank you very much for taking the time to meet me today. I enjoyed our discussion, and I'm now even more excited about the possibility of working for ABC and joining your team.

It was great to learn that you are embracing technology as it relates to your business – both in terms of day-to-day operations and the future delivery of ABC's programmes (eg, on-the-spot training). I am very interested in, and have an affinity for, computer technology and would love to be a part of your efforts in this area.

As we established, I have related experience in all of the required areas for the position. Establishing the new system for the delivery of assessment workshops to your key clients would be an exciting project, and one that recent experience suggests I can handle effectively.

I remain very interested in the position, and I look forward to hearing from you soon. If you require additional information in the meantime, I can be reached on 12345 678910.

Yours sincerely,

Marcy Smith
12345 678910

Follow-up e-mail (after face-to-face meeting) (librarian)

The interview in this case was by a committee and very structured, leaving the applicant with the feeling that there was more she would have liked to have said. This thank-you letter conveys some of these ideas. The result: the applicant was hired for this high-level position.

From: Mary Kelner [mkelner@email.com]
To: Recipient's e-mail address
Cc:
Subject: Librarian selection meeting, Monday pm

Dear Recipient's Name,

Thank you for the opportunity to meet you and the selection committee on Monday. I enjoyed our discussion of the Director of Library Development opening. I was impressed with your vision for this individual's role.

Based on our conversation, I believe that I possess the capabilities to meet your expectations for this key position with the Library Service.

To reiterate the experiences I bring to this opportunity, please note the following:

- Promoting programmes and fostering working relationships with over 1,000 member libraries in all major segments of the field. These activities also encompass extensive community outreach.
- Providing strategic vision and mission, and motivating staff to pursue visionary goals. In two leadership assignments, I have recognized staff for their efforts and given them the guidance and direction that has delivered exceptional programme results.
- Managing capital projects and spearheading information technology initiatives. These encompassed upgrades to comply with access requirements, renovations that improved the use of space, and leading efforts to incorporate technology into library settings.
- Supervising departments in urban and suburban settings to address a broad range of competing priorities. Among these experiences was the supervision of an Interlibrary Loan department serving 100 individual branches in a five-county area.

I am most interested in this position and am confident that my track record at XYZ demonstrates my capacity to 'hit the ground running', and apply my leadership, enthusiasm and expertise to furthering the mission of the Library Service in this development role. I look forward to continuing our discussions in the near future.

Yours sincerely,

Mary Kelner
0123456 7890

Follow-up e-mail (after face-to-face meeting) (executive assistant)

From: Janice Moss [jmoss@email.com]
To: Recipient's e-mail address
Cc:
Subject: CEO's PA interview follow-up

Dear Recipient's Name,

The time I spent being interviewed by you and Sandra gave me a clear picture of your company's operation as well as your corporate environment. I want to thank you, in particular, Phillip, for the thorough picture you painted of your CEO's needs and work style.

I left our meeting feeling very enthusiastic about the scope of the position as well as its close match to my abilities and work style. After reviewing your comments, Phillip, I think the key strengths that I can offer your CEO in achieving his agenda are:

- experience in effectively dealing with senior level staff in a manner that facilitates decision making;

- proven ability to anticipate an executive's needs and present viable options to consider;

- excellent communication skills – particularly, the ability to gain feedback from staff and summarize succinctly.

Whether the needs at hand involve meeting planning, office administration, scheduling or just serving as a sounding board, I bring a combination of highly effective 'people skills' and diversified business experience to deal with changing situations.

With my energetic work style, I believe that I am an excellent match for this unique position. I welcome an additional meeting to elaborate on my background and how I can assist your CEO.

Yours sincerely,

Janice Moss
0123456 7890

Follow-up e-mail (after face-to-face meeting) (management information systems)

From: Christopher Falk [cfalk@email.com]
To: Recipient's e-mail address
Cc:
Subject: Great meeting

Dear Recipient's Name,

Thank you for meeting me this morning. Our associate, _____, assured me that a meeting with you would be productive, and it was. I sincerely appreciate your counsel, insight and advice.

I have attached my CV for your review. I would appreciate any feedback you might have regarding effectiveness and strength. I understand you may not have any searches under way that would be suitable for me at this time, but I would appreciate any future considerations.

As we reviewed this morning, I seek and am qualified for senior MIS positions in a medium to large high-tech manufacturing or services business. I seek a salary in the £150,000-and-above range and look to report directly to the business CEO. These requirements are somewhat flexible depending on a number of factors, especially potential, of a new position. My family and I are willing to relocate to any area.

Thanks again, and please let me know if I can be of service to you. I wish you and your colleagues continued success and look forward to a business relationship in the future.

Yours sincerely,

Christopher Falk
0123456 7890
Attachment: CV

Follow-up letter (after face-to-face meeting) (assistant)

MELANIE SHREVE
1 Any Street
Anytown AA1 1AA
12345 678910

(Date)

Emily _____
(Title)
ABC Ltd
1 Industry Plaza
Anytown AA1 1AA

Dear Ms _____,

Thank you for the opportunity to discuss the position of Personal Assistant with you yesterday afternoon.

ABC Ltd is involved in one of the most pressing concerns of today: environmentally safe methods of disposing of solid waste materials. The challenge of creating proper disposal systems is paramount. I look forward to being a part of an organization that is focusing on furthering the technology needed to enhance our environment.

The skills that I have to offer you are:

- professionalism, organization and maturity;
- excellent office skills;
- ability to work independently;
- a creative work attitude;
- research and writing skills;
- varied business background;
- willingness to learn.

At ABC Ltd I would be:

- a productive assistant to management;
- part of a technologically developing industry;
- in a position to learn and grow with the opportunities presented by your company;
- involved in the excitement of a new, expanding company.

Again, thank you for considering my qualifications to become a part of your organization.

Yours sincerely,

Melanie Shreve

Melanie Shreve

Follow-up e-mail (after face-to-face meeting) (sales)

This letter is a follow-up to a meeting Carol arranged with a targeted employer. While there was no position currently available, she nevertheless wants to 'sell' her suitability.

From: Carol Ann Conasta [caconasta@email.com]
To: Recipient's e-mail address
Cc:
Subject: Great to meet you on Wednesday

Dear Philip,

First of all, thank you. I thoroughly enjoyed our meeting last Wednesday, and greatly appreciate your insight and the time taken to discuss where I might best fit in to the ABC team. Your professionalism and willingness to share what you know put me instantly at ease, and I am now even more motivated to be part of ABC's success.

Let me begin by restating how flattered I am that you saw such potential in me. I likewise feel confident that I have the management and leadership expertise, marketing skills, and business development experience to be successful, and I see tremendous opportunities for ABC in the future.

However, as we discussed, I understand that my first step is to make my mark as a member of the Road Crew and am equally excited at the opportunity to make an impact on the front line. I realize that you are not currently in the position to make such an offer, but I want to re-emphasize my enthusiasm to join the ABC team wherever you feel I could add value.

I'd like to re-state three key points:

- I possess the drive, commitment and strong people skills required to make an impact in this industry.
- I offer proven business development, sales and revenue-building experience.
- I know what it takes to get results, both from myself and from others, and have proven again and again to be the 'go to' person when results are expected.

I hope that you and I have the opportunity to continue our discussions and, once again, I appreciate the time you spent meeting me. I wish you continued success in all your efforts and look forward to seeing you at the Sales Excellence seminar at the end of July.

Yours sincerely,

Carol Ann Conasta

Carol Ann Conasta
0123456 7890

Follow-up e-mail (after face-to-face meeting) (general)

From: William Long [w_long@hotmail.com]
To: Recipient's e-mail address
Cc:
Subject: eMarketing strategy meeting follow-up

Dear Recipient's Name,

I appreciate the time you took today interviewing me for the position. I hope our two-hour meeting did not throw off the rest of the day's timetable. I trust you will agree that it was time well spent, as I sensed we connected on every major point discussed.

Your insight on e-commerce was intriguing. My history in hi-tech, manufacturing and biomedical industries and background in technology solutions seems to be a good match with the opportunities available in your company. As I mentioned, at XYZ Biomedical I initiated the marketing strategies that opened our markets to South America. What I failed to mention is that I also have contacts with some e-commerce investors developing online portals targeted at the South American market.

I am very interested in the position and would like to contact you on Tuesday to see where we stand.

Yours sincerely,

William Long
12345 678910

Follow-up e-mail (after face-to-face meeting) (sales manager)

From: Damien Chavez [salespro@aol.com]
To: Recipient's e-mail address
Cc:
Subject: Thanks for an exciting meeting. Next steps?

Dear Recipient's Name,

I thoroughly enjoyed our meeting on Wednesday. After learning more about ABC Ltd and its goals, the prospect of joining the organization as the Western Region Sales Manager is even more exciting.

One of the most important things I have learned in my 20+ years in sales is to listen to what the customer needs. I have always taken pride in designing customized solutions that not only meet the clients' objectives, but are also competitive in price. This philosophy has enabled me to exceed corporate expectations for 17 consecutive years.

In addition, I have managed to convert about 65 per cent of my clients into established accounts, an objective you indicated was a high priority for your sales team in ensuring the company's continued growth.

I recognize that ABC Ltd's Western Region Sales Manager position is an important cornerstone in the company's overall growth plans for the new fiscal year. The company is poised to make significant strides to gain ground on the competition and the territory will be instrumental in making the corporate goals a reality. I am excited about contributing my expertise, meeting ABC's customers and building long-term client relationships.

Thanks again for your time. I am certain that I can be a valuable asset to your sales team, and I look forward to having the opportunity to contribute to ABC's growth.

Yours sincerely,

Damien Chavez
12345 678910

Follow-up e-mail (after face-to-face meeting) (senior counsellor)

This e-mail shows how her skills and experience in counselling matched this particular job opening and would be an asset to the agency and its clients.

From: Susan Goodman [skilledcounsellor@earthlink.net]
To: Recipient's e-mail address
Cc:
Subject: Looking forward to next week

Dear Recipient's Name,

I would like to thank you for affording me the opportunity to meet you to discuss the Senior Counsellor position with your organization. I have long been an admirer of your services and commitment to the community. I am very confident that my education, experience and counselling skills will enable me to make an immediate and long-term contribution to your mental health programme.

The position we discussed seems well suited to my strengths and skills. My counselling and teaching background includes an emphasis on the family unit and its influence and relationship to each client's therapy.

I am looking forward to seeing you, again, next week. If you require any additional information before then, please feel free to call. Thank you for your time and consideration.

Yours sincerely,

Susan Goodman
12345 678910

Follow-up e-mail (after face-to-face meeting) (management)

From: Henry Jacobs [hjacobs@yahoo.com]
To: Recipient's e-mail address
Cc:
Subject: The right choice for programme development

Dear Recipient's Name,

The programme development position we discussed on Friday is a tremendously challenging one. After considering your comments about the job requirements, I am convinced that I can make an immediate contribution toward the growth and profitability of ABC Ltd.

Since you are going to reach a decision quickly, I would like to mention the following points, which I feel qualify me for the job we discussed:

1   Proven ability to generate fresh ideas and creative solutions to difficult problems
2   9 years' experience in the area of programme planning and development
3   Ability to manage successfully many projects at the same time
4   A facility for working effectively with people at all levels of management
5   Experience in administration, general management and presentations
6   An intense desire to do an outstanding job in anything I undertake

Thank you for the time and courtesy extended to me. I look forward to hearing from you.

Yours sincerely,

Henry Jacobs
12345 678910

Follow-up e-mail (after face-to-face meeting with a recruitment professional) (general)

From: Joseph Winger [jwinger@hotmail.com]
To: Recipient's e-mail address
Cc:
Subject: Thanks for the meeting

Dear Recipient's Name,

It was a pleasure meeting you in your office last week. I appreciate the time you spent with me, as well as the valuable information you offered. As we discussed, I have adjusted my CV in regard to my position with _____. I have attached the new CV with this e-mail so that your files can be updated.

_____, please allow me to thank you again for the compliment on my ability to present a strong interview. Please keep this in mind when considering me for placement with one of your clients.

Yours sincerely,

Joseph Winger
12345 678910
Attachment: CV

Follow-up e-mail (after face-to-face meeting) (entry-level)

From: Dana Sorrensen [dsorrensen@mindspring.com]
To: Recipient's e-mail address
Cc:
Subject: Thank you for the meeting

Dear Recipient's Name,

I would like to take this opportunity to thank you for the interview on Wednesday morning at _____, and to confirm my strong interest in an entry-level Customer Service position with your company.

As we discussed, I feel that my education and background have provided me with an understanding of business operations that will prove to be an asset to your company. Additionally, I have always been considered a hard worker and a dependable, loyal employee. I am confident that I can make a valuable contribution to your Group Pension Fund area.

I look forward to meeting you again in the near future to discuss the next steps. I am sincerely interested in and enthusiastic about the position.

Yours sincerely,

Dana Sorrensen
12345 678910

Follow-up e-mail (after face-to-face meeting) (auditing)

From: Alex Davis [auditpro@earthlink.net]
To: Recipient's e-mail address
Cc:
Subject: Very motivated by our meeting

Dear Recipient's Name,

Thank you for allowing me the opportunity to meet you to discuss the IT Audit position currently available at ABC. The position sounds very challenging and rewarding, with ample room for growth. I feel my background and qualifications have prepared me well for the IT Audit position we discussed:

- five bulletted
- points reviewing
- key skills, qualifications
- and experience
- relating to the post.

I am committed to the ongoing development of my audit skills and feel I could work well with your focused audit staff at ABC. I am very interested in coming in to meet the team and to move on to the next step. I look forward to hearing from you.

Yours sincerely,

Alex Davis
12345 678910

Follow-up e-mail (after face-to-face meeting with a recruitment professional) (banker)

From: Your Name [Your e-mail address]
To: Recipient's e-mail address
Cc:
Subject: Banker, headhunter follow-up

Dear Recipient's Name,

I understand that the search is continuing for the Market Manager position at _____ .
As you continue your search, I would like to ask that you keep my accomplishments and experiences in mind:

1 Direct experience in all phases of commercial banking, including: market segmentation, prospecting, building and maintaining customer relationships, lending, and the sale of non-credit products and services.

2 Captured 24 per cent share of public funds market within 2 years, and captured a 22 per cent share of insurance company funds market.

3 Developed cash management and trust products tailored to the needs of my target market; £55 million in sales in 3 years.

4 Marketed services through e-mail, social networking, investor-specific seminars, and through active participation in target market's industry professional organizations.

5 Maximized relationships and increased balances through the sale of trust and cash management products.

I will call you next week, after you have seen the other candidates, to continue our discussion. In the meantime, please be assured of both my competence and commitment.

Sincerely,

Your Name
01234 567890
Attachment: CV

Follow-up e-mail (after face-to-face meeting) (senior executive assistant)

From: Your Name [Your e-mail address]
To: Recipient's e-mail address
Cc:
Subject: Senior Executive Assistant Meeting

Dear Recipient's Name,

I want to express my appreciation to you and your team for the time and courtesy extended to me during my interview on _____ . I enjoyed the discussions and am even more enthusiastic about the Senior Executive Assistant position at _____ .

I recognize the importance of the Senior Executive Assistant's role, and based on my past successes I am confident that I can meet the challenge. My educational background is strong and includes an MBA degree with a major in Marketing, plus many hours of continuing professional education.

Likewise, my work experience and skills in administrative duties, calendar management, budgeting, data management, risk management, and research and planning would permit me to make some valuable contributions to your team. Specifically, my experience includes:

- Ability to anticipate the executive's needs and proactively bring together resources to support executive in addressing issues.
- Facility for working effectively with people at all levels of management and cross-functional teams on a global basis.
- High level of confidentiality, professionalism, and sound judgement.
- Employee training and development.
- Experience in administration, general management, and presentations.
- Proven ability to generate fresh ideas and creative solutions to difficult problems.
- Ability to manage multiple projects successfully in fast-paced environments.

I was impressed by the warm and confident professionalism of your team and look forward to moving our conversations forward to their logical conclusion. I am excited about the opportunity and I want to join the team as your next Senior Executive Assistant. Please do not hesitate to contact me at 0123456 7890 or emailaddress@yourserver.net.

Yours sincerely,

Your Name
01234 567890

'Resurrection' e-mail (HR position)

Although Kenyon didn't get the job, he wants to keep the lines of communication open and hopes to be considered for other positions.

From: Kenyon Stewart [kstewart@email.com]
To: Recipient's e-mail address
Cc:
Subject: Director of Human Resources Position

Dear Eric,

Congratulations on the selection of your new Director of Human Resources! I hope this new person meets your expectations and I wish you every success.

I appreciate the chance to apply for the position and am grateful for the consideration you have given me throughout this process. Although I am obviously disappointed at not being the successful applicant, I remain interested in potential opportunities with ABC. If for any reason you decide it is necessary to reopen the search at any time, please be aware that I am still interested.

In the meantime, should there be openings for support positions within the HR Department, or positions in other departments, I would like to be considered for such opportunities. I know my organizational skills, communication skills and flexibility would make me an asset to any organization. If you know of other openings I would be most appreciative if you could pass that information on to me.

Thank you for all your time and consideration. I look forward to speaking to you again soon.

Yours sincerely,

Kenyon Stewart
01234 567890

'Resurrection' letter (team director position)

Another applicant was selected for the position that Madison was interviewed for. Because he hopes for other opportunities, he wants to both thank ABC for the interview and keep his name (and qualifications) at the top of their mind for future consideration.

Madison P Aldridge

1 Any Street
Anytown AA1 1AA
12345 678910

12 January 20–

Michael Anderson
ABC Ltd
111 Any Avenue
Anytown AA1 1AA

Dear Mr Anderson,

Thank you for the opportunity to attend the interview for the Team Director position. I genuinely appreciated the chance to discuss your vision for the DEF programme.

Although another candidate was ultimately selected for this important position, I was pleased to be among the short list of applicants under consideration.

As we have discussed, I believe that my nine years' experience with XYZ provides me with a wealth of knowledge and expertise that can be beneficial to ABC. I continue to be committed to the mission of the DEF programme, but also wish to offer myself as a candidate for other roles where my capabilities can further the objectives of ABC.

To briefly reiterate, some of the qualities that I can bring to a new position include:

- **strategic vision, creative energy and strong leadership skills;**
- **capacity to build collaborative teams across public, private and government sectors;**
- **excellent project management capabilities;**
- **ability to build employee morale and inspire team members to strive for excellence;**
- **innovative problem-solving skills.**

Please keep me in mind if other opportunities should arise where my talents would be an asset, particularly as you move ahead with implementation of the DEF project. I would enjoy speaking to you further to discuss how I can best serve ABC's needs.

Thank you, again, for your consideration.

Yours sincerely,

Madison P Aldridge

Madison P Aldridge

'Resurrection' e-mail (stevedore)

This is a follow-up e-mail to several telephone conversations with the best contact within the target company, the company director.

From: Casey Smith [csmith@email.com]
To: Recipient's e-mail address
Cc:
Subject: Thank you

Dear Mr Roberts,

First, I want to thank you for the time you spent with me in recent telephone conversations. I know you are a very busy person.

On 4 August I attended the recruiting event at the Convention Centre. I submitted my CV and spoke very briefly with a representative. In the short time I chatted with her I did my best to communicate my interest in, and qualifications for, the job. However, due to the overwhelming number of applicants there just wasn't sufficient time to convey how qualified I really am.

With that in mind, I have attached my CV for your review. To summarize:

- I have an extensive history of working safely around heavy equipment.
- I am in outstanding physical condition.
- I am a very reliable and dedicated employee.
- I have received first aid, CPR and terrorism awareness training.

This CV is only a hint of who I am – words on paper cannot replace a personal conversation. Therefore, would you please consider my request for a face-to-face interview so that you may evaluate my qualifications, abilities, drive and enthusiasm for yourself?

I will make myself available for any time that you can take out of your schedule. Thank you for your consideration, and I look forward to meeting you if possible in the near future.

Yours sincerely,

Casey Smith
0123456 7890
Attached: CV

'Resurrection' letter (social worker)

Having already been interviewed by Mr Thornson, Beth started the letter in an upbeat, informal manner to re-establish a rapport. The indication that he thought she was well suited at the time of their initial interview was an effective way to sell herself.

BETH ANDERSEN
1 Any Street
Anytown AA1 1AA
12345 678910
BAndersen@4kidsake.net

16 February 20–

Mr William Thornson
Foster Care and Adoption Coordinator
BAAF
111 Any Avenue
Anytown AA1 1AA

Dear Mr Thornson,

I bumped into Mr O'Brien yesterday and learned that St Mary's is opening a new foster care division this coming March. One thing led to another, and he informed me that BAAF is in desperate need of social workers and foster/adoptive care counsellors to fill several positions.

You might not recall my name, but I hope I can help you to remember our meeting. I participated in an interview with you in early May of 20– for the position of Foster Care Counsellor with BAAF's Brentwood facility. We discussed my involvement with St John's Youth & Family Counselling Programme at great length, and agreed I would be well suited to a similar position with BAAF as an Adoptive Care Counsellor. Unfortunately, funding was reduced that month leaving BAAF with no other choice but to put a freeze on hiring.

As you can imagine, I am thrilled to learn of BAAF's new foster care programme, and would welcome the opportunity to meet again to pick up where we left off. For your convenience, I am enclosing my updated CV for your review.

Thank you for your reconsideration. I look forward to hearing from you soon.

Yours sincerely,

Beth Andersen

Beth Andersen
Enclosure: CV

'Resurrection' e-mail (manager's position)

From: Leanne Boardman [lboardman@email.com]
To: Recipient's e-mail address
Cc:
Subject: Manager position

Dear Recipient's Name,

I understand from _____ of _____ that the search is continuing for the Manager position at _____ ABC Bank. As you continue your search, I would like to ask that you keep in mind the following accomplishments and experiences that I would bring to the job:

- Maximized relationships and increased balances through the sale of trust and cash management products.
- Captured largest share of public funds market in _____ within three years and captured a disproportionate market share of insurance companies in _____ .
- Developed cash management and trust products tailored to the needs of my target market.
- Marketed services through mass mailings and brochures, through planning and conducting industry-specific seminars, and through active participation in target markets' industry professional organization.
- Direct experience in all phases of commercial banking, including: market segmentation, prospecting, building and maintaining customer relationships, lending, and the sale of non-credit products and services.

Yours sincerely,

Leanne Boardman
0123456 7890

'Resurrection' e-mail (construction manager)

From: Eric L Ross [elross@email.com]
To: Recipient's e-mail address
Cc:
Subject: Construction Management searches?

Dear Recipient's Name,

I am in the construction management and business management fields and I am writing to follow up a CV I sent a while ago. Perhaps you did not have any active searches that met my qualifications or my file was mislaid.

I am still in the market for an executive position that matches my qualifications and abilities. I am open to relocating throughout the United Kingdom and overseas. If any positions become available, I would be interested in hearing from you. Thank you for your consideration. I'll call you in a couple of days to follow-up.

Yours sincerely,

Eric L Ross
0123456 7890
Attachment: CV

'Resurrection' letter (entry level)

Elizabeth A Andrews

1 Any Street • Anytown AA1 1AA

(Date)

Bob _____
(Title)
A,B&C
Executive Search Consultants
111 Any Avenue
Anytown AA1 1AA

Dear Mr _____,

I feel I should explain more thoroughly why I am willing to take even an entry-level position considering all my past experience. And that's just it – past experience.

For the past three years I ran my own small business, which, of course, kept me out of the job market. Meanwhile, computers took over the world! Fortunately, since moving here and doing temp jobs, I have gained hands-on experience in data entry. I have also taken and finished a private course in Microsoft Word. So I believe that makes me computer literate, if not entirely experienced.

Nevertheless, I'm in no position to be disdainful of clerical jobs, as I realize I must start somewhere. Fortunately, I enjoy all facets of office work (even filing), so that would not be a problem. I have enough faith in myself and my ability to learn quickly to know that some form of upper movement would be possible for me… eventually.

Incidentally, even though I am on a temp job this week and possibly next, I do have an answering machine I check every couple of hours during the day. So please leave a message and I'll return your call soon after.

Thank you, and I look forward to hearing from you. I have enclosed another copy of my CV for you.

Yours sincerely,

Elizabeth Andrews

Elizabeth Andrews

Enclosure: CV

'Resurrection' e-mail (account executive)

From: Katherine Knockwood [accountexecutive@aol.com]
To: Recipient's e-mail address
Cc:
Subject: Thanks from Katherine, I'll be the next one

Dear Recipient's Name,

I wanted to thank you for the interview we had on 13 March 20–. The position that was being offered sounds like something I would be interested in. However, I do understand your reasons for not choosing me for the position, and I thank you very much for your honesty.

Perhaps when you are looking for an account executive with five years' experience instead of ten, you will bear me in mind. I am determined to be your choice. I hope the fact that I came a close second to someone with twice my chronological experience will help you remember me.

I look forward to hearing from you, and thank you again for your time. With your permission I will stay in touch.

Yours sincerely,

Katherine Knockwood
12345 678910

'Resurrection' e-mail (programmer)

From: Robert Zelinski [programmerpro@yahoo.com]
To: Recipient's e-mail address
Cc:
Subject: Lost in the shuffle?

Dear Recipient's Name,

I must have been one of the first people you spoke to about the Programmer job posting, because at the time you seemed very interested, as I was. However, when I called you back, you had received so many calls for the position, you didn't know one from the other. That's understandable, so I hope I can stir your memory and, more important, your interest.

I have a solid programming and project development background in both the Windows and Macintosh worlds and have worked in web applications for 5 years now. What's even better is my hobby: my work. I spend countless hours in one way or another doing things that concern computing.

You had some ideas for children's software and thought having kids would help when working on such software. You had asked if I had children and I do: a four-and-a-half-year-old daughter and a four-and-a-half-month-old daughter. My oldest uses _____ on my Macintosh at home and double-clicks away without any assistance from my wife or myself. She has learned a great deal from 'playing' with it and is already more computer literate than I ever expected. We need more software like _____ to help stir the minds of our children.

I have attached a CV for your perusal. But in case you don't want to read all the details, here it is in short:

- I have six years' programming and development experience in Windows.
- I have three years' programming and development experience on the Macintosh.
- I am currently the Senior Developer for Macintosh programming here at _____ Ltd
- I have 2 years' experience working extensively on cloud-based applications.

I look forward to speaking to you again, so please don't hesitate to call me, either at home (12345 678910) or at work (109876 54321) anytime.

Regards,

Robert Zelinski
12345 678910

'Resurrection' e-mail (product manager)

From: Amanda Jones [ajones@hotmail.com]
To: Recipient's e-mail address
Cc:
Subject: You were right

Dear Recipient's Name,

Four months ago you and I discussed an opportunity at Active Products, and you were kind enough to set up meetings with _____ and _____. Shortly thereafter, as you know, I accepted a position with _____, where I am now.

For reasons I will go into when we meet, I would like to reopen our discussions. If you think such a conversation would be mutually beneficial, I hope we can get together. I'll call next week to see when you have a half hour or so of free time.

Yours sincerely,

Amanda Jones
12345 678910

Rejection of offer letter (head librarian)

Tamara has decided to take another position. As a courtesy, she wants to tell Anytown Library that she's no longer interested in the position, while keeping her name alive for any future opportunities.

Tamara L Salinger

1 Any Street • Anytown AA1 1AA • 12345 678910

12 January 20–

Mr Henry O Felix
Anytown Library Services
111 Any Avenue
Anytown AA1 1AA

Dear Mr Felix,

Thank you for taking the time to meet me recently to discuss the position of Head Librarian. I genuinely appreciated the opportunity to meet the Committee to learn about the position. I was very favourably impressed with the Anytown Library System and believe that if selected, my contributions would have significantly enhanced your organization's success.

However, I am writing to ask that my name be withdrawn from further consideration for the position at this time. I have recently been offered another challenging and rewarding opportunity. The relative time-frames involved have made it necessary for me to make a decision without further delay, and I have chosen to accept the offer.

Had circumstances permitted, I believe that it would have been productive to continue our discussions and am confident that we could have arrived at a mutually beneficial arrangement. I would be most interested in applying for the position should there ever be another search for a Head Librarian at some future date.

I wish you the best of luck in your current search, and much success in the future. Thank you, again, for your time and consideration.

Yours sincerely,

Tamara L Salinger

Tamara L Salinger

Rejection of offer letter (team supervisor)

This candidate was interviewed for a position that turned out to be below his level of experience and at a salary well below his expectations. He didn't want to slam the door shut on other opportunities but couldn't accept the position offered.

Ms Lucretia A Selander
Programme Director
ABC Ltd
111 Any Avenue
Anytown AA1 1AA

Dear Ms Selander,

Thank you for your e-mail message updating me on the status of the telecommunications project we discussed in our recent telephone conversation.

Although I genuinely appreciate your consideration for the Team Supervisor position, at this time, I feel it is in my best interest to seek a position more closely aligned with my level of experience and demonstrated managerial skills.

I remain most interested in opportunities with ABC, and ask that you keep my name under consideration for other positions that would more fully capitalize on my knowledge and expertise.

Thank you for your time and interest.

Yours sincerely,

Christopher J Franz

Christopher J Franz

Rejection of offer letter (general)

AUDREY M LAURENCE
1 Any Street • Anytown AA1 1AA
12345 678910 • alaurence@rochester.rr.com

(Date)

Phillip _____
(Title)
ABC Ltd
1 Industry Plaza
Anytown AA1 1AA

Dear Mr _____,

It was indeed a pleasure meeting you and your staff to discuss your needs for a
_____. Our time together was most enjoyable and informative.

As we have discussed during our meetings, I believe the purpose of preliminary interviews is
to explore areas of mutual interest and to assess the fit between the individual and the position.
After careful thought, I have decided to withdraw from consideration for the position.

My decision is based upon the fact that I have accepted a position elsewhere that is very suited to
my qualifications and experiences.

I want to thank you for interviewing me and giving me the opportunity to learn more about your
company. You have a fine team, and I would have enjoyed working with you.

Best wishes to you and your staff.

Yours sincerely,

Audrey Laurence

Audrey Laurence

Rejection of offer e-mail (department manager)

From: Allen Meriden [managementpro@earthlink.net]
To: Recipient's e-mail address
Cc:
Subject: With regret for the present and sincere hope for the future

Dear Recipient's Name,

I would like to take this opportunity to thank you for the interview on Thursday morning, and to express my strong interest in future employment with your organization.

While I appreciate very much your offer for the position of Department Manager, I feel that at this stage of my career I am seeking greater challenges and advancement than the Department level is able to provide. Having worked in _____ management for over four years, I am confident that my skills will be best applied in a position with more responsibility and accountability.

As we discussed, I look forward to talking to you again in January about how I might contribute to ABC in the capacity of Unit Manager.

Yours sincerely,

Allen Meriden
12345 678910

Acceptance letter (marketing research manager)

JULIE GREGORIO
1 Any Street
Anytown AA1 1AA
12345 678910

(Date)

Ms Emily _____
ABC Financial Services Group
1 Industry Plaza
Anytown AA1 1AA

Dear Ms _____,

Thank you for your positive response to the Marketing Research Manager position. I am delighted to accept your offer of employment and look forward to 'jumping in head first' into the various projects we discussed during our meetings, especially sales forecasting and strategic market planning for ABC's core product line.

I am honoured that your organization feels that I am the right person to lead your marketing research efforts, and I am confident that I can deliver the results ABC wants. As I mentioned in our telephone conversation yesterday, I am constantly in touch with what the competition is doing with the goal of placing my team's effort higher in the marketplace to yield maximum results.

As you request, I will contact Mary Smith, Human Resources Manager, on Monday morning to arrange an orientation appointment. I look forward to meeting you after that to discuss in detail my ideas for meeting the objectives we explored in our interviews.

Yours sincerely,

Julie Gregorio

Julie Gregorio

Acceptance letter (managing consultant)

Jacqueline Mains
1 Any Street ▪ Anytown AA1 1AA
12345 678910 Home ▪ managingconsultant@comcast.com

(Date)

Dear Philip,

I want to thank you for the privilege of joining your staff as Managing Consultant. Your flexibility and cooperation in the counter negotiations was encouraging. Thank you for making every effort to make the pending transition a smooth one.

As you request, I am providing this letter, for my official file.

'In that your organization is a competitor of my previous employer, and in that this organization seeks to maintain goodwill and high levels of integrity within the industry, it should be duly noted, that neither you nor any representative of your organization, sought me as a prospective employee. It was my identification of a possible position, and solely my pursuits toward your company, that resulted in my resignation as Senior Director, to join your firm as Managing Consultant.'

If I can provide additional clarification on this matter, or assist in protecting the ethics of your company, please notify me. I look forward to starting with your team on the 15th of July.

Yours sincerely,

Jacqueline Mains

Jacqueline Mains

Acceptance letter (director)

·· **Victor L Williams**
1 Any Street
Anytown AA1 1AA

(Date)

Emily _____
(Title)
ABC Ltd
1 Industry Plaza
Anytown AA1 1AA

Dear Ms _____,

This letter will serve as my formal acceptance of your offer to join your firm as Director of _____. I understand and accept the conditions of employment that you explained in your recent letter.

I will contact your personnel department this week to request any paperwork I might complete for their records prior to my starting date. Also, I will arrange a physical examination for insurance purposes. I would appreciate your forwarding any reading material you feel might hasten my initiation into the affairs of _____.

Yesterday I tendered my resignation at _____ and worked out a mutually acceptable notice time of four weeks, which should allow me ample time to finalize my business and personal affairs here and be ready for work at _____ on schedule.

You, your board and your staff have been most professional and helpful throughout this hiring process. I eagerly anticipate joining the ABC team and look forward to many new challenges. Thank you for your confidence and support.

Yours sincerely,

Victor L Williams

Victor L Williams

Acceptance e-mail (general)

From: George Keller [gkeller@mindspring.com]
To: Recipient's e-mail address
Cc:
Subject: Yes! Absolutely! I accept!

Dear Recipient's Name,

I would like to express my appreciation for your letter offering me the position of
_____ in your _____ Department at a starting salary of
£53,000 per year.

I was very impressed with the personnel and facilities at your company in Anytown and am
writing to confirm my acceptance of your offer. If it is acceptable to you I will report to work on
20 November 20–.

Let me once again express my appreciation for your offer and my excitement about joining your
engineering staff. I look forward to my association with ABC and feel my contributions will be in
line with your goals of growth and continued success for the company.

Yours sincerely,

George Keller
12345 678910

Negotiation letter (general)

Betsy Kimble

1 Any Street	12345 678910
Anytown AA1 1AA	bkimble@aox.com

(date)

Mr Philip _____
(Title)
ABC Ltd
1 Industry Place
Anytown AA1 1AA

Dear Philip,

I want to thank you for your invitation to join ABC. I have reviewed the offer of the position and salary, as presented in your letter dated _____. I would like to ask for clarification on a few items prior to providing you with a 'formal acceptance'. While none of these items are necessarily 'deal breakers', I believe they will enable both parties to begin the partnership more informed about mutual goals and expectations.

As per the breakdown provided:

- I accept the bonus scheme as proposed.
- I accept the paid holiday and personal days plan as proposed.
- I accept the educational reimbursement plan as proposed.
- I accept the Direct Payroll Deposit plan as proposed (if elected).
- I accept the Medical, Dental, Pension and Life Insurance benefits as proposed, contingent on factors clarified below.

Points of Clarification:

- What is available in regard to 'Share Options'?
- What are the 'standard hours of operation' for ABC employees?
- Would it be possible to have a 'Performance Evaluation' at the end of six months?
- I would like to structure the holiday entitlement as follows: Three days in remainder of year 20–, One week during calendar year 20–, Two weeks during calendar years 20– to 20–, Three weeks beginning January 20–.
- In light of the 'out-of-pocket expenses' anticipated, how might we agree to get the annual base salary to £35,000? I am open to a number of different options to achieve this goal, including profit sharing, commission or 5 per cent annual bonus arrangement.

Page 1 of 2

Betsy Kimble
Page 1 of 2

I am excited about the long-term possibilities that exist at ABC. As you can see by my level of interest, I intend to be with you for a long tenure of success. I believe my skills will be an enhancement to the existing leadership. My presence will enable you and others to focus on new aspects of business development and achieve corporate goals and objectives that will be beneficial to us all. Again, I want to thank you for the gracious offer. I look forward to finalizing these minor details very soon.

Yours sincerely,

Betsy Kimble

Betsy Kimble

Negotiation letter (sales)

Eden Miller
1 Any Street • Anytown AA1 1AA • 12345 678910 • e-mail: salespro@anyserver.co.uk

(Date)

Dear Mr _____,

I have reviewed your letter and the specific breakdown regarding compensation. I believe there to be a few items to clarify, prior to providing you with a formal acceptance. I do not consider any of the items to be 'deal breakers' in any way. I also do not perceive them to be issues that cannot be discussed, as we are in fact, moving ahead.

The primary concern has to do with the commission structure, as opposed to salary plus commission, to which I have grown accustomed. I am therefore asking for a one-time initial payment to me in the amount of £5,000. I am trying to diminish some of the 'exposure' that I may experience in the transition from one office to another. I also believe exposure will be felt as a shift occurs from receipt of compensation on a monthly basis, when I am currently accustomed to a biweekly format. Lastly, I am hoping to afford your company the opportunity to share some of the 'risk' in this process and show some 'short-term good faith' toward what I hope will be a long-term relationship of success, productivity and increased profitability.

The second clarification revolves around the bonus scheme: the percentages, timeframes and terms. This is something we can discuss over the course of the next two weeks. You may even be able to pass something specific on to me in writing.

With these two concerns articulated, I want you to know that I will be meeting the owner of our company tomorrow morning, to discuss my plans for departure. In fairness to him and to my current client load, I could not start full-time with you for 21 days.

I would like to set a time for us to have dinner one evening next week, so you can meet my wife and we can talk a bit less formally.

Looking forward to what lies ahead,

Eden Miller

Eden Miller

Negotiation letter (senior lab specialist)

MITCHELL T NORDSTROM

1 Any Street • Anytown AA1 1AA

12345 678910 (days) / 01987 654321 (evenings) • labspecialist@cs.com

(date)

Philip _____

ABC

1 Industry Plaza

Anytown AA1 1AA

Dear Philip,

I want to thank you for the time that we were able to spend together last week. I was encouraged by the invitation to join ABC as Senior Lab Specialist. The position, responsibility and geography are consistent with my career goals and objectives. Based on the information that you gave to me, there are a number of items for clarification, prior to providing you with a formal acceptance. None of the items listed are necessarily 'deal breakers', but they are essential to us beginning this tenure with full disclosure of mutual expectations and responsibilities. Items for clarification are as follows:

- Detailed description of insurance benefits.
- Realistic analysis of the company share and bonus scheme.
- Written explanation of educational reimbursement allowance.
- The mobility plan seems very reasonable, but would like specifics on the Permanent Work Relocation. (Is it an allowance or reimbursement of actual expenses incurred in the move?)
- Detailed explanation of the Variable Pay Plan.

This final item is significant, as it will have an impact on the full compensation potential and modify the suggested salary. In our conversations, I communicated to you that I was making £32K while working part-time and going to college. The salary offer is substantially lower and represents a pay cut. My goal is to discern how feasible it will be for me to meet my financial obligations.

I am interested in your company and this position, but am finding it difficult to give serious consideration to anything less than £40K salary plus benefits. I am hoping to discover a variety of vehicles that will enable you to help me achieve that goal, so that I can help you accomplish your growth and profit targets.

I look forward to discussing these issues with you in the very near future and trust that we will soon be working together in the best interest of Philip _____, Mitchell Nordstrom, and ABC Ltd.

Yours sincerely,

Mitchell Nordstrom

Mitchell Nordstrom

Negotiation letter (product specialist)

MARY A MARTIN

0198765 4321 (Mobile) • 12345 678910 (Home)
productspecialist@email.com
1 Any Street • Anytown AA1 1AA

(Date)

Philip _____
(Title)
ABC Ltd
1 Industry Plaza
Anytown AA1 1AA

RE: Product Specialist/ABC Team

Dear Philip,

Thank you for your offer of employment with ABC Ltd. Your state-of-the-art company would afford me the opportunity to make a contribution while continuing to grow professionally in an ever-evolving industry. I am confident that my strong work ethic would enhance the ABC Team.

As you know from our previous conversations, I have outstanding skills and abilities that I can bring to ABC. First and foremost is my hands-on experience in the medical field. I have a proven track record of relating well to other medical professionals and accommodating their needs. It is my understanding that as Product Specialist, my expert communication skills will be essential to performance success. With my experience in troubleshooting technical problems, I know that technology can be learned but becomes useful only when it can be translated into user effectiveness. My expertise integrates both of these critical components that are key to the Product Specialist role.

The Product Specialist position promises challenge and a high level of professional commitment that I am prepared to embrace. However, based upon the value I can bring ABC, plus the knowledge that the annual salary range for this type of position in our industry normally falls between £34,000 and £46,000, I must request that you reconsider your starting offer of £35,000. I am more than happy to assume all the responsibilities necessary to meet the expectations of the Product Specialist position at a starting salary of £40,000. Of course, I appreciate the generous benefits package that you provide.

I look forward to your response, and hope that we can reach an agreement that will enable me to begin my career with ABC on 4 June.

Yours sincerely,

Mary Martin

Mary Martin

Resignation letter (ITU nurse)

This situation was sensitive. A lot of names and dates were needed to explain the events leading to the decision to resign. Notice how Elizabeth apologizes so she doesn't burn her bridges.

Elizabeth Dixon, RN

1 Any Street ▪ Anytown AA1 1AA ▪ 12345 678910 ▪ criticalcare@med.net

26 April 20–

Ms Dorothy Powell
Director of Special Care
ABC Hospital
111 Any Avenue
Anytown AA1 1AA

Dear Ms Powell,

As requested by Joan Larson, Nursing Manager, I am submitting this letter as written confirmation of my resignation as a per-diem on-call ITU nurse with ABC Hospital.

My employment with ABC was scheduled to begin on 7th April as a permanent part-time ITU nurse; however, in the interim, I accepted a permanent full-time position with XYZ Hospital to begin on 1st May. On 3rd April I met with Gretchen Miller, Human Resources Administrator, to inform her of my decision. I expressed a desire to honour my commitment with the understanding that the need for flexibility in my schedule would be taken into consideration. Ms Miller contacted Joan Larson to discuss an alternative employment arrangement. Subsequently, my status of permanent part-time was changed to per-diem on-call.

Immediately upon completion of the mandatory two-week orientation period, I was faced with a schedule conflict. As a result of an apparent miscommunication, I was scheduled to do my floor orientation from 21st April to the 25th. I approached Diane Willis, Nursing Manager, to resolve the conflict and learned that she was completely unaware of both my situation and agreement between Joan Larson, Human Resources, and myself. As a result, my resignation seemed to be the logical solution.

Ms Powell, it was never my intention to cause you administrative problems; therefore, please accept my apology for any inconvenience experienced. Thank you for the opportunity to be a part of your staff.

Yours sincerely,

Elizabeth Dixon

Elizabeth Dixon

Resignation letter (care coordinator)

Marilyn was offered a new position with another organization, and this letter helped her make a positive exit from her current employer.

Marilyn Cummings

1 Any Street
Anytown AA1 1AA
12345 678910

9 April 20–

Ms Karen Lawrence, RN
Patient Care Manager
Community Care Centre
111 Any Avenue
Anytown AA1 1AA

Dear Karen,

This letter will confirm my resignation from the position of Care Coordinator. I have accepted a new position as Supervisor of Client Services at a growing medical centre in London.

My last day of employment will be on Friday, 9 May 20–, which should provide sufficient time to complete existing projects and assist with the transition to a new coordinator.

The past 10 years at the Centre have been both professionally and personally rewarding. Thank you for your trust and support over the years. I have appreciated the opportunity to expand my skills and work with many talented individuals.

Yours sincerely,

Marilyn Cummings

Marilyn Cummings

Resignation letter (management)

This is a very firm resignation, where a company needs encouragement to live up to obligations.

ROBERT McINTYRE
1 Any Street
Anytown AA1 1AA

home: 12345 678910
mobile: 0198765 4321
robertmcintyre@crpn.com

11 November 20–

Tim Johnson
Title
XTC Ltd
111 Any Avenue
Anytown AA1 1AA

Dear Mr Johnson,

I am writing this letter as a follow-up to the resignation notice I submitted on Wednesday, 5 November 20–. Given the sensitive nature of the events leading to my resignation, I feel it is in everyone's best interest to resolve any issues remaining as quickly as possible.

In this respect, I hope that you will demonstrate swift compliance in delivering to me the management severance package guaranteed as a result of my employment with your firm. I wish to move ahead in my career and put the past few months behind me, as I am sure you can understand; therefore, I am certain you will act upon this request in a professional and forthright manner.

Please be advised that, in the event that there is an attempt to withhold or deny this severance package to me, I will have no other alternative but to seek legal remedy for this situation. **Again, I believe that you will act with integrity concerning this issue**, and I only mention the possibility of legal action in the unlikely event that my request is rejected or delayed.

I can assure you that I, like you, would like for this to be resolved without further complications or additional steps – and as quickly as possible.

Mr Johnson, I thank you in advance for your swift attention and cooperation in this matter.

Yours sincerely,

Robert McIntyre

Robert McIntyre

Resignation letter (sales representative)

·· **Gerard Carlisle**

(Date)

Phillip _____
(Title)
ABC Ltd
1 Industry Plaza
Anytown AA1 1AA

Dear Mr _____,

Please accept my resignation of my position as Sales Representative in the _____ area, effective 25 January 20–. I am offering two weeks' notice so that my territory can be serviced effectively during the transition, with the least amount of inconvenience to our clients.

While I have very much enjoyed working under your direction, I find now that I have an opportunity to develop my career in areas that are more in line with my long-term goals. I thank you for the sales training that I have received under your supervision. It is largely due to the excellent experience I gained working for ABC that I am now able to pursue this growth opportunity.

During the next two weeks, I am willing to help you in any way to make the transition as smooth as possible. This includes assisting in recruiting and training my replacement in the _____ territory. Please let me know if there is anything specific that you would like me to do.

Again, it has been a pleasure working as a part of your group.

Best regards,

Gerard Carlisle

Gerard Carlisle

··
1 Any Street • Anytown AA1 1AA • 12345 678910

Resignation letter (director)

David R Chang

1 Any Street, Anytown AA1 1AA / 12345 678901
chang@earthlink.com

(Date)

Emily _____
(Title)
ABC Ltd
1 Industry Plaza
Anytown AA1 1AA

Dear Ms _____,

As of this date, I am formally extending my resignation as _____. I have accepted a position as Director of _____ at a university medical centre in _____.

My decision to leave ABC was made after long and careful consideration of all factors affecting the company, my family and my career. Although I regret leaving many friends here, I feel that the change will be beneficial to all parties. My subordinate is readily able to handle the company's operations until you find a suitable replacement. I intend to finalize my business and personal affairs here over the next few weeks and will discuss a mutually acceptable leaving date with you in person.

Finally, I can only express my sincere appreciation to you and the entire board for all your support, cooperation, and encouragement over the past years. I will always remember my stay at ABC for the personal growth it afforded and for the numerous friendships engendered.

Yours sincerely,

David Chang

David Chang

Resignation e-mail (general)

From: John Billingsly [systemsoperator@hotmail.com]
To: Recipient's e-mail address
Cc:
Subject: With regrets but many thanks

Dear Recipient's Name,

This e-mail is to notify you that I am resigning my position with ABC effective Saturday, 26 March 20–.

I have enjoyed my work here very much and want to thank you and the rest of the MIS Department for all the encouragement and support you have always given me. In order to achieve the career goals that I've set for myself, I am accepting a higher level Systems Operator position with another company. This position will give me an opportunity to become more involved in the technical aspects of setting up networking systems.

Please know that I am available to help with any staff training or offer assistance in any way that will make my departure as easy as possible for the department. I want to wish everyone the best of luck for the future.

Yours sincerely,

John Billingsly
12345 678910

Thank-you letter (after success) (general)

Matilda Vixard
1 Any Street ▪ Anytown AA1 1AA ▪ 12345 678910

(Date)

Phillip _____
(Title)
ABC Ltd
1 Industry Plaza
Anytown AA1 1AA

Dear Mr _____,

I want you to be among the first to know that my job search has come to a very successful conclusion. I have accepted the position of _____ Director at _____ Ltd, located in _____.

I appreciate all the help and support you have provided over the last few months. It has made the job search process much easier. I look forward to staying in contact with you. Please let me know if I can be of any assistance to you in the future. Thank you.

Yours sincerely,

Matilda Vixard

Matilda Vixard

Thank-you e-mail (software manager)

From: Shane Franklin [softwarespecialist@yahoo.com]
To: Recipient's e-mail address
Cc:
Subject: Great News! Thanks for the help!

Dear Recipient's Name,

I am happy to inform you that I received and accepted an offer of employment just after Christmas. I am now employed by _____ Ltd.

I would also like to thank you for all your help the past few months not only in my search for employment but also for your understanding and friendly words of encouragement.

My duties include responsibility for all accounting software (General Ledger, Accounts Payable, Accounts Receivable and Fixed Assets) for _____ worldwide plus the first-year training of several entry-level employees.

I am enjoying my new responsibility and being fully employed again, although at times I feel overwhelmed with all I have to learn.

If there is ever anything I can do for you, please call me. I hope you and your family had a wonderful Christmas and I wish you much luck and happiness in the new year.

Yours sincerely,

Shane Franklin
12345 678910

INDEX

Find out more at www.koganpage.com/ultimatecareers
Twitter updates #ultimatecareers
@koganpage